THE CODES OF
DIVINE LOVE

THE CODES OF DIVINE LOVE

A CHANNELED TEXT

CHRISTINA RICE

GOLDEN
HOUR
PUBLISHING

Published and distributed by Golden Hour Publishing.

Rice, Christina
The Codes of Divine Love

Library of Congress Control Number: 2024904346

Paperback 978-1-959513-08-7

Hardcover 978-1-959513-09-4

eBook 978-1-959513-10-0

To my soul family—thank you for teaching me divine love.

CONTENTS

INTRODUCTION

What really is love? The feeling we all crave. The feeling we all seek. The invisible force that moves us, drives us, inspires us, pushes us, transforms us, breaks us, and heals us. The place from which our inspiration flows. It's what we read books about, watch movies about, listen to songs about, daydream about, and obsess about. It's at the epicenter of everything we do. Why do we crave it so deeply? Because it's who we really are.

We spend so much of our lives thinking about love, talking about love, and desiring love, but do we really know what we are looking for? It's the thing I've been curious about most in my life, but I never got anywhere satisfactory with that exploration until I started developing my own spiritual connection. Through that journey, I started to understand love in a different way. I started to question what I grew up thinking "love" really was, and what society told me it was. Are the ways in which we relate to each other, communicate with each other, and respond to each other really love? I guess it depends on who you're talking to. The more time I spent doing energy work, meditating, and channeling, I felt a distinct frequency that I could only describe as love. But it was a different kind of love. It felt...

divine. It felt like soaring. I started to wonder if what I thought was love in other situations was really love at all. As I channeled more and more information about the concept of love and about relationships themselves, I started to create a new understanding for myself—one that felt true and authentic for me.

I've always been fascinated with human interactions—it's what led to my obsession with books, film, psychology, sociology, and spirituality throughout my life. One aspect of human interaction I've always been most curious about has been relationship skills. What does it mean to have good relationship skills? How are they cultivated? When it comes to life skills that many of us are never formally taught, some of those, in my opinion, include how to communicate clearly, how to address conflict in a loving way, what healthy boundaries look like, and what healthy relationships look like. The question is—who gets to decide that? How do we judge that? There are outlines for what that means in many different places, but does it really serve us to follow those? Personally, I was taught many of those outlines at a young age, growing up in a religious setting. But it wasn't until I dove deep into my own trauma healing and shadow work as an adult that I started to realize there was so much I needed to learn. I realized that true relationship skills, like clear communication and healthy boundaries, were never really taught to me. I started to recognize that so much of what I thought was normal was not necessarily healthy. I had to unlearn. And then I got to learn. I am continuing to learn, every day.

Growing up, I always felt like an outsider. I felt like there was a slight disconnect between me and other people. For that reason, I never knew if I would find real love—in friendships or romantic relationships. It's in relationships that we really see all our fears and wounds on display. For a very long time, it was extremely difficult for me to open up. As someone who is generally very communicative and probably a bit too much of an open book with people I hardly know, I would completely shut down whenever anyone got too close. I was so afraid of my heart getting broken that I put walls around it. In doing so, I just created what I was trying to avoid in the first place—loneliness.

That loneliness haunted me, like a dark cloud hanging over my head. So I decided to dive into it—what would it take for me to create truly loving, vulnerable relationships? I had to understand myself, and then share that with the people around me. I had to love myself, first. So I did. I spent a few years focusing strictly on my own inner healing, exploring everything I didn't like about myself, every shadow, everything I was scared of, everything I didn't want to face. I got to know all of myself, deeply. I learned to accept myself, and eventually—I fell in love with myself. I fell in love with the process of getting to know myself—a lifelong journey. I committed to myself—to being authentic, to choosing myself, and to trusting myself. The cloud lifted. I didn't feel lonely anymore. From there, sharing my heart felt natural. When I committed to being fully myself, sharing that, and showing up in relationships in the way I wanted to be met, everything changed.

I have found so much freedom and happiness in my life from exploring the underlying assumptions, expectations, and beliefs I've had about myself, others, and how the world works. The more I've laid it all out in front of me, the more I've realized how many things I decided were true that didn't have to be, and how many of those stories were leaving me feeling powerless, anxious, sad, or disconnected. The more I've explored topics from an energetic perspective, it's created space for me to bring those beliefs and behaviors to light in a loving way, from a neutral perspective, to simply observe what's serving me and what's not. Coming from that place of curiosity has helped me see myself and others with so much more compassion and love, and it's from that place that I've created so many deep, truly loving connections that I am endlessly grateful for. I didn't know those types of connections were even possible.

People are craving true connection now more than ever before. They are recognizing the division agenda and ready to move beyond it. They are realizing how many illusions, stories, and programs have been affecting our relationships and breaking down our connections to each other. People are realizing that neither hyper-independence nor codependence are really fulfilling our desires on a core level. We are ready to know and experience true love. We are ready to put our egos aside and manifest the divine love we really want. But do we really know how to connect in a healthy way? How to love? What are we really looking for? How can we, if we've become disconnected from ourselves? If we're ready to create something new on this planet, what will relationships really look like?

This book is a trance channeled text that unpacks love itself and how we can experience divine love. This is the second installment in a series from the Monarch Being, a high-frequency entity that I experience as a stream of divine feminine energy surrounded by a vortex of divine masculine energy, flowing through and around me. The Monarch Being has been one of my most expansive teachers in the last few years—challenging my beliefs, helping me see different perspectives, and inviting me to see beyond the duality of good or bad, right or wrong.

As with all channeled texts, and all information in general, it's important to read it as simply a perspective. Take what resonates and leave what doesn't. It doesn't have to be truth for you. Tune into what resonates for you, on a soul level. Channeling different beings has taught me how to receive information without giving my power away. Channeled information is an interesting perspective that offers me valuable reflection points and a way to explore my own beliefs, but it doesn't have to be my own opinion. Channeling has taught me to receive new perspectives with an honest, open heart, and to notice if anything triggers me. In the places where I feel triggered, pushed, and uncomfortable, I see where that perspective might be bumping up against my ego, and that is where I've learned the most about myself, my underlying beliefs, my fears, and the stories I've held onto.

If you have not already read the previous installment in the series, I would recommend first reading *Manifestation Mastery: How to Shift Your Reality & Co-Create with the Universe*. This book very much builds on that text, where they define and explain many terms and concepts used in this book. If you decide to skip that advice, and if this is your first channeled text, I'll offer a few disclaimers. First, you might notice that the language sounds a bit different from other books. The Monarch Being doesn't always follow proper grammar or standard rules of language. Each word is chosen and each sentence phrased specifically in order to create a frequency transfer. Concepts and phrases are repeated as a way to work the message into your energy body, past your logical brain. This allows you to receive more than just what your brain is expecting or ready to process. In other words, it helps the ideas get past resistance so you can actually feel into them, in case there's something valuable in there for you. You don't necessarily have to understand the content to receive the information. That is one of the things I love the most about a channeled text—it unlocks your own inner knowing. You might notice that as you read the book, many of your own insights or memories drop in. Whether or not it seems related, it all is. This book will unlock whatever you need to know that is connected to the topic. Don't be surprised if your relationships start to naturally change while you're reading this book.

There are so many different layers to channeled texts—the content you read, the vibrational transfer of information, the activation codes, and the energy within. You'll get something different out of it every time you read it. The text really is alive. Because an energy is being transferred, you might feel energy flowing through you as you read. You might feel heat, cold, tingles, vibrations, or different sensations in your body. The frequency that is transferred through the text is really more important than the words themselves. It's everything beneath the surface that is most activating. This text is meant to activate you to divine love in your own life. If you want that to happen, all you need to do is allow it. I recommend taking your time with the text, receiving all you can from it, and reading it as many times as you feel called to. It really will be a completely different experience each time.

I feel this information is coming through at such an important time—we are ready for more. People are tired of settling for fine. We want incredible. We want epic. We want divine. We want love, but is that really how we're relating to each other? It's time we get very clear on the world we want to create, and how we are each playing our part in creating it. We are all co-creators. This book shifted me in powerful ways, and continues to each time I read it. It has called me out and called me up in important ways. It has healed deep parts of me that I didn't know were still hurting. It has completely shifted the way I view all types of relationships. It has reminded me that I do have the power to create the things I desire in my life. It has helped me take responsibility for myself and how I am showing up. It has reminded me that my soul is always guiding me to miracles. It has reminded me just how much one person can affect so many others through embodying love. It has taught me just how much love can heal us all. It has reminded me that love is as powerful and fierce as it is gentle and kind. It is the foundation on which I hope we can co-create this next chapter of the world, together.

I hope you receive the love in this transmission as fully as I did.

Show up with an open mind and heart, and you'll receive more than you could have hoped for.

THE CODES OF
DIVINE LOVE

Activating
Divine Love

CHAPTER 1

THE DEFINITION OF DIVINE LOVE

We would like to begin with an invitation—to read this text and to receive this transmission with an open heart. It will be required for you to receive this text with an open heart if you wish to fully understand what is within and what can be activated within you. When we describe love, we are referring to the divine definition of love—love in its truest, purest vibrational form. That definition of love, this understanding of love as we explain it, might be different from your own. If it differs from your own, it is not to say one definition or perspective is right and one is wrong—it is simply so you understand what we are referring to, and we invite you to explore the definition we offer throughout this text. Give it a chance.

The invitation to come with an open heart is not just for reading this text—an open heart is also that which is required for you to fully receive the love you seek. We will offer a loving warning that there might be points in this text that poke at wounds and trigger a re-evaluation of relationships in your life. There might be moments within this text where you do not like the conversation, and we ask you to explore within yourself—why? What tender place is it touching? What wound, what belief, what fear is this hitting? For if nothing else, at least use this text to allow a deeper uncovering of yourself, to allow yourself to bring all of your beliefs, your fears, your conditioning, and your own definitions to light—to see it all laid out on the table—for this is what vibrational "work" is. It is an opportunity to make what is unconscious conscious and bring all to light. It is only when you are able to fully see the truth of what is that you can find freedom. It is only when you allow yourselves to see the truth of what is that you are living love. Truth is love.

Allow this information to help you uncover your own truths, or, perhaps, where you have been living from beliefs and patterns that are not your truth. This is an opportunity to explore yourself, not an invitation to take on everything that is offered in this text as your own. This is where you will start to understand love for yourself more fully—remembering the power within. Trusting yourself. Consuming a new perspective from a place of curiosity, but not giving your power away in the process of its consumption. Tuning into what resonates for you, taking the pieces that land, and exploring the pieces that don't, or maybe setting them aside. There is value in everything. Where you judge the information in itself, where you push away what you do not like with an energy of frustration or bitterness or annoyance—is this living as love?

From that invitation, we will be clear that we will not be filtering our perspective (by that we mean we will not be calibrating to yours), and we hope you understand that what is conveyed is coming from a place of so much love. Direct communication is love. The path to unlocking and remembering the divine love within you, the love that you so desperately wish to taste again, that you feel within you but sometimes struggle to allow to fill you up, although sometimes you forget this is your true essence—this path will require you to look in places that you might not be comfortable with, and to pull apart the tense energies within you so you may find love once more. We send love to these tender places, but we will be clear in that the purpose of this transmission is to be quite plain when it comes to the understanding of divine love.

Many of you run around constantly seeking it—love. You write about it, you listen to songs about it, you watch movies about it, you daydream about it, you talk about it—so much of your culture is centered around finding love. In this obsession, its definition has been confused. That was not unintentional, but to keep you chasing. To keep you in lack. To keep you in an illusion of separation. In a space of forgetfulness. But when you feel into this longing within and the depth of the yearning—when you allow yourself to fully feel it—this is the indication that it is your birthright. The longing is so deep because it is your truth. It is the call within to return to who you really are. Because everything else does not feel resonant. Everything else does not feel enough. Because it is not. Because love is your soul memory. It is the purest version of you. It is where you come from. It is who you are at your core. That longing within is your indication—this is not something foreign to you, and it is not something that only the lucky few find. It is an indication of your inner knowing that it is yours. It is your truth. It is who you are. Anything else will not do.

It is when you settle for what is less than divine love that you constantly feel misaligned in your system. You see health issues arise from this—body aches, physical pain, recurring symptoms, chronic disease—and you feel anger toward more situations than you might expect. You feel anxiety and depression. There are so many places where this misalignment shows up. The truth is—it is where you are not feeling connected to love. It is the illusion that you are disconnected from divine love that makes you sick. It is the illusion that you are disconnected from divine love that leads to you giving your power away to others. It is the illusion that you are disconnected from love that keeps you chasing something outside of yourself. The illusion tempts you into settling. When you remember, when you claim your essence as divine love, and when you live as love, you remember your power. Love can truly move mountains. It is the divine healer. It is the most powerful force of all. There have been many in "control" who wish to drive this illusion of disconnection. This is done through your mainstream media—movies, books, social media content—all feeding the illusion of what love is and what it is not, what it looks like, how you find it, what it feels like, what is right and wrong about it. The way in which "love" has been portrayed in much of your society is not, in fact, a representation of love as we define it.

We invite you to wipe the slate clean. Come into this exploration with a beginner's mindset. Otherwise, you will be battling the conditioning, your ego, and your mind the whole way through. This new understanding of love will challenge what you have been taught and what you have been modeled. It will challenge what your family, friends, and partners might have expressed to you, or what they expect of you. But for you to truly access these divine codes and come back home to yourself, you must decide to wipe the slate clean. You must decide to give yourself the chance to recreate the definition for yourself. It is only through more of you doing this and living the divine definition of love, resetting the standards and shifting the norm, that others will wake up to the memory.

Love is a force powerful beyond measure. Think of how it motivates. Think of how it moves people to do what they never thought possible—the superhuman strength to lift a car to save a loved one. The complete transformation of an unhealthy lifestyle overnight, to show up for the ones you love. The complete chaos it can create within one's body, mind, and soul. An invisible force that is so powerful. If it has the power to break you down, imagine how it has the power to build you up. Imagine, if all were powered by divine love—the purest definition, the truest essence—what could be created? What could be healed? If you created all from the divine love that is within you, how would the world change? It is the return to love that will set you free. But it all starts with authenticity.

CHAPTER 2

SHIFTING HOW YOU RELATE

When we speak of love, we speak of a vibration—a frequency. It is flow. It is pure. It is oneness. It is the embodiment of your purest expression as an extension of Source. As you read this text and receive the codes, you will feel it. As you read this text and start to make shifts in your life to lead with love, you will feel it. You have accessed this frequency many times, for it lives within you, and it is what you were created from. It is the purest form of your essence—everything else is conditioning, hypnosis, amnesia. Your truth is love. Love heals. Love creates. Love transforms. When we speak of this frequency, it is something that runs through you. It is a frequency that can be embedded in any consciousness, in the essence of any thing, but also in the energetic cords and energetic dynamics between you and those around you. We have many angles to explore—you, friendships, romantic partnerships, family, and other types of relationships.

In order for the dynamic to shift between you and the world around you, as you see it from this energetic place, it all starts with you. It is all from within. It will be required for you to start to live as the energy of divine love, and from this it is infused into all that you do. When this occurs, this is what you attract. It will be required that as you live from this vibration, you maintain it. That you see through the illusions of what is not truth—what is not love. This is the power of love—it cuts through illusions. It dissolves what is not truth. This, in fact, is why so many avoid it. You seek it, and you do desperately desire it, because your soul knows it is truth, and that it is the access point to everything you have ever desired. In fact, it is the only thing you have ever desired. But you also "fear" it, or so you think. This is the ego, not wishing to see the truth—because what will happen on the other side?

Once you know the truth, there is no going back. So you create dissonance within the system. Your soul is pure love, divine love, but you also resist it, because you are afraid to let the illusions dissolve. What is on the other side? What will it mean when you admit to yourself how you truly feel, or what you truly desire? Which relationships are not serving you? We hope you understand this is being conveyed from a neutral perspective. This will transform the way you view every relationship in your life so you can see each with more clarity. For most who read this, it will shake their foundation—but the foundation can only crack if it was unstable to begin with.

Are you ready to see what is solid and stable? Are you ready to see what was built on a foundation of divine love? What is will not be broken—it is the strongest force of all. But what is not will come to light. As you live as love, it will be made clear which dynamics in your life are not rooted in love. These codes are crucial at this time, because you are feeling called to shift. The first part of this shift started on a more individual level, but the next phase of the shift will require a drastic change in how you relate. Many of you have been doing very well in realigning with your own truth, living your own truth, and stepping further into your authenticity. Many of you are taking the invitation to explore the depths of yourselves, your multidimensionality—and this has been a beautiful process! How beautiful it is to step into the courage to explore the light and shadow, to learn to love all of yourself, and to bring to light your illusions, limiting beliefs, and where you are holding yourself back. We are so excited that so many of you have stepped up to this exploration, have shifted the way in which you live and think, and have turned what was automatic into consciously living and thinking. This has been a beautiful shift within each of you, and the beauty of the journey is that this is an ongoing process, as all of life's experiences offer you opportunities to explore and get to know yourself.

However, the next part of the puzzle is to shift how you relate. Many of you have shifted the way in which you talk to yourselves, although we will touch more on that, but the shift has not been threaded into your dynamics with "others," who, for clarity's sake, are other aspects of you, as an extension of the One. For ease in communication in this text, however, we will be using terms that refer to "others" in order to explore these dynamics, but it is important to remember that how you relate to others is also how you relate to yourself! Here you find a mirror. When you pay attention to how you speak to others, where you judge others, and what you think of others, ask yourself what this mirrors about your own relationship to yourself, what you believe about yourself, and how you speak to yourself. There is always a connection.

This external reality is a playground for you—a place where you can uncover more from within yourself. This is how you understand yourself more deeply—through connection. Through the mirrors available all around you, in "others"—"other" extensions of Source that reflect to you that which you do not see yourself. How can you truly know what you look like without a mirror? These connections allow you to see more angles of yourself. These mirrors are your doorway to more clearly embodying your highest truth, your clearest authentic code, and this is where you are fully connected to your essence as an extension of Source. It is through your connections to others that you are able to explore more of yourself, and it is also where you anchor in your vibration through how you act and how you relate. If you have truly made an energetic shift, if you are truly living as love, the way you relate will shift. The more you live as the embodiment of love, as your most authentic self, you will relate differently. If you are still relating the same, then either the action is not following the energetic shift, and so it is not yet fully ingrained, or the energetic shift has not yet been made. In either case, light is shed to see the truth.

We return to the importance of the shift in dynamic between you and the other. Do you believe that the collective is truly operating from a place of unconditional love and forgiveness right now? At the time of this transmission, it is not. We will be clear—you are more ready to make shifts within yourself than in how you relate to others because you do not always want the dynamic with others to shift. You do not want to upset others, you do not want to have to release relationships, you do not want to deal with the drama, you do not want to admit that something must go, you do not want to admit that you desire more, or something else. You are hiding. In doing so, you are robbing yourself of your truest happiness. You are robbing others of their truest happiness. You are forgetting your divinity. You are giving your power away. You are settling. And if you feel that kernel of truth deep within your gut, you are already one step ahead. Acknowledging your truth opens the gate to your freedom.

And so, you cannot be afraid to rock the boat. You are afraid to rock the boat by being, exuding, living divine love? If there is any way to rock the boat, it is with love! It feels better for everyone, in the long run. It dissolves what is not true, and when you are living in untruths, you are caged. You are a prisoner to fear. This is misalignment in your system. This is dis-ease. This manifests as anxiety. This manifests as worry. Your body's wisdom tells you what you need to know. Do not settle, for it will only make you sick.

And when we say do not settle, of course you get to choose—but choose consciously. Make an informed choice. Living from love is a commitment to the truth of what is. It is a commitment to being responsible for your energy field. When you pretend to not know, when you pretend to be okay when you're not, this is not love. If you wish to make the shifts within yourself, but not make shifts in how you relate to others, then you are not truly making the shifts within yourself, as aligned action will follow the vibrational shift. From what frequency does the action, the way in which you relate, come from? As your vibration gets higher, so must that of your relationships, and so, dynamics will recalibrate. If they are not, you are still anchored.

CHAPTER 3

UNCONDITIONAL LOVE

We will return to the phrase unconditional love. We think it is interesting that in your society, there is a differentiation between love and unconditional love. When we refer to love, if we were to remove any adjectives, love is naturally unconditional. And so, in the adjective itself, we see the mismatch in definition—where there has become a difference between unconditional love and conditional love. If it is conditional, is it love? Well, according to your normalized definition, or commonplace understanding of the word, many of you might believe so. But from our perspective, it is not. And so, this is where we disrupt the definition itself, and we invite you to ponder this for yourself. From this exploration, you might wish to use this word more cautiously in some scenarios, and in others, more loosely. You will understand this as we continue.

To love with condition, what does this mean? We understand that underneath this is the idea that if someone were to betray you, to hurt you, to harm you, to break whatever contract you have in place, then the love would end. There is a condition to the love. "I love you as long as you don't..." And that way of thinking can be immature in some cases. "I love you as long as you do everything I say," for example. In other cases, it comes from an intention of respect for self—"I love you as long as you do not break the terms of our commitment to one another through lying, cheating, infidelity..." and so on. But the question becomes—does the love itself end? Or does it shift form? Does the love itself end, or are different boundaries set in place? Does the love end, or do you learn? Must the love end simply because the relationship has shifted form? If the contract is complete, must this mean the love is complete as well? We see these as separate choices.

For here is where we will touch on what it would mean to live in a world of unconditional love (as we understand it, love itself)—the response is simply different. To live in a world of unconditional love is to love your neighbor. It is to love your best friend, your partner, your parents, but also the person that hurt you. This does not mean the person who hurt you needs to be an active part of your life, and it does not mean you need to move forward as if nothing happened, but it would look like seeing them fully. Seeing them for who they really are—an extension of Source, as well. Seeing them for who they really are—love, even if conditioning, fear, and pain have clouded their vision. It is to see with compassion. It might feel easy to see from anger, fear, or rage, but when seeing from this lens, you vibrate at this lens yourself. You operate from this lens yourself. And so, for you to see another from a place of anger, you are choosing anger. To choose love for yourself is to see others from a lens of love.

When there is resistance to this idea, we understand, but we also invite you to not make up stories about what this means. Again, it is not to say that whatever occurred was "okay." It is not to say that what was done was loving, when clearly that was not the vibration. Do not forget your power to transmute. To meet anger with more anger simply feeds more of that in your system, and on the planet. To meet anger with love is how you transmute the lower frequencies. It is how you heal. Can you view fear and anger from the lens of love? This is how you transmute it. Your feelings are your truth!

There are times when you feel hurt or betrayed. When you feel your heart break. When you feel as though you cannot live another day, you cannot get up another day, and you have no idea how you will move forward. Yet somehow, you do. This is the love that lives inside you. This is the powerful force of love that drives you, that moves you. Love heals you. Love is the light inside that will never go out. Even when you feel clouded with darkness, it is the dim candle that will never lose its burn. When you remember that, you can look for it. You will find it, and you can choose to fuel its flame, and allow it to fill you up. Allow that to be your guiding light. From there, you are able to take a step forward, even if it is just one step at a time. And you move forward, even though you thought you could not before. It is what you choose to act on. It is how you choose to see the world. You can choose love, or not.

In fact, to choose love will mean releasing relationships from your reality. Setting a boundary, or releasing a relationship, can be done with and from anger, fear, avoidance, or love. When you orient yourself from this vibration, the answer becomes clear.

We will point out what might seem to be a harsh truth—many of you have not experienced many relationships, if any, in this incarnation that are purely rooted in unconditional love—the truest form. What most of you think is love is obligation or addiction. What many of you think is love is simply commitment. Commitment is beautiful, and love can include commitment, but they are not the same. You can love someone and not be committed to a relationship with them. You can commit to a relationship with someone and not fully relate to them from a place of divine love. But when you anchor from divine love, commitment to someone or something, when you choose it, is effortless. It naturally follows.

We will also point out that just because someone says something or does something that feels hurtful does not necessarily mean there is no love. This can be where someone has forgotten their truth. This is the tricky thing about your human experience—so many opportunities to fall into illusion. This is where you explore the dynamics of living from your ego versus living from your soul. When the overall frequency of the energetic cord is divine love, when the vibration of the relationship itself is divine love, in a moment where one falls into an illusion, it is met with love and forgiveness, and the illusion is dissolved. From there, you have a completely different experience, and the word "conflict" might not feel as resonant anymore. What was a "fight" or a "heated discussion" before might actually become an expansive exploration and an opportunity for growth, because you are not looking to make someone else wrong. You are not looking to make yourself right. You are not looking to prove a point. You are not anchored from comparison energy. You are genuinely seeing the love in all.

CHAPTER 4

CONNECTING WITH DIVINE LOVE

How do you connect with the frequency of divine love? You have felt it. Reflect on the moments—the moments when you have felt so deeply seen, held, and loved. The moments themselves. Reflect on the moments when you realized there was something so much bigger than your mind and ego. The moments when you saw the true beauty in the world, in yourself, in another. When you were connected to pure beauty, pure pleasure, and pure joy. Divine love is playful! It is fun! It is creative! When you are connected to the divine, this is love. Many of you feel this connection when you create space to tune into Source itself, the Oneness, or however you identify with it. We are talking about when you connect with the essence of unconditional love— where everything is from—and remember yourself as an extension of this. When you are connected to the Source, truth is all that can exist. You know that you will only be met with love. That your fears will dissolve. That you are always held. That there is nothing that would change that feeling, of connecting with Source—for it is love. And that is within you, always.

Start to recognize the different types of "love" that you have experienced, and ask yourself—which of these was unconditional? Which of these was unconditional in its dedication to seeing the real me—a being of love? That is love. And what were the others? Obligation? Commitment? Exploration? Lust? Addiction? Jealousy? Fascination? Desperation? Outsourcing? Longing? Partnership?

Take time each day to intentionally connect with the Source of love—with the vibration itself. That is your comparison point. You might think, how can a human compare with this? Isn't that an unfair comparison? An unfair expectation?

Is it? Or is that your conditioning? Is it not an unfair expectation that others cannot and will not embody their divinity? Is it not an unfair expectation and assumption that others will not embody the divine love that lives within them? Isn't it unfair to allow others to settle for what is less than their truth? To enable them to live in illusions? To enable them to cap their potential? Isn't it unfair to lower the standards for everyone, rather than hold them higher, creating space for all to live their truth, as love? Is it too much to expect others to be their most authentic selves—which is love? We see it as your birthright to be reminded that of course you are meant to act as love and from love. To normalize anything else is where you are feeding the cycle of dis-ease, of codependency, of unhealthy attachment.

If you knew your best friend could win the Olympics, would you lovingly encourage them to go for it, or would you recommend they not even try? If your best friend could be a world-class singer, would you tell them to hide their singing voice at home, or encourage them to share it with the world for all to experience? If your best friend had a million-dollar idea, would you tell them to explore it, to go for it, or to stay quiet? And what of you, if you were in the other position? Would you want your best friend to hold the vision with you? Would you want your best friend to encourage you to step into the most authentic, most powerful, most expanded version of yourself, the version of you that is living a life you genuinely love? Or to expect that you could never achieve your dreams? Would you want them to choose the no instead of opening the door to step into the yes? Where have you already decided it isn't possible? Where have you already decided to stay in unnecessary limitations that you created for yourself?

Notice where your own fears and negative self-talk get projected onto others. Notice where that of another gets projected onto you. What would it look like to release the projections, and to commit to truth? To commit to love?

Holding the greater vision is love. Holding the vibration of love and inviting others to step into it as well is love. This is simply holding the frequency of truth. From there, it is up to others what they decide. But it is not love to rob others of their opportunity to decide.

CHAPTER 5

SHOWING
ANOTHER WAY

What if you can be the one to show another way? So many feel trapped, and they are desperate to shift that feeling. Why is this? You know what you know. You know what you are around. You know what you grew up around. Many are operating from conditioning rather than the infinite information available to them at higher frequencies. Most simply have not seen another way. They are not aware of it. They have not experienced it. It is the same with your relationships. You will think codependency is love if you have not experienced anything else. You will think the color blue is the color green if you have been told it is green your whole life, until you bump into someone else who tells you it's blue. You anchor into whatever you have been told or modeled from a young age until you experience something different and give yourself the opportunity to explore if that could be another way of doing things.

This is why you must hold the vibration—to support more of the collective in experiencing that frequency. It is like instantly waking up from hypnosis, waking up from a trance, and wondering how you even got there. This is illumination. Love dissolves illusions. Love wakes you up. Love is how you access truth. Love heals. Truth is love. Love is truth. Love is honesty. Where you are not being honest with yourself or another is where you are not living love. Holding the frequency of love is love, of course. If you are holding a lower vibration, how can you say that is love? Recognize the frequency you're holding. Recognize the frequency you are embodying. Recognize the vibration you are allowing. Is settling love? Is letting someone walk all over you love? Not for anyone involved, as we see it. When you justify choices from a place of not wanting to rock the boat, understand that this excuse is not love. That can be your choice if you want it to be, but understand what the frequency of it is.

This will call you up into your next level of expansion. This is from love. We love you so much that we want you to see another way. We want you to explore another perspective. We do not want you to settle for anything less than what you deserve, for it is what you are—love! As so many of you are looking for it and chasing it, we would like to point out that it is difficult to find something when you don't really know what it is. Really, it is difficult to find something when you think it looks like something it doesn't.

You think you found it, and then you get involved, and then it falls apart, and then you stop believing in it. You have a poor experience in a relationship and you stop believing in love. You wonder if it really exists. Well, it's not love's fault. Was that really love? That is the question. When you are chasing it from someone or something else, you are missing the point. As with everything you wish to attract, you first must find it within yourself, and then live from this vibration. From there, your external reality calibrates to you. You attract more of what vibrates at this frequency. And so, the first step is recognizing it within yourself, then letting the frequency fill you up, and then living from that frequency. It is first to understand that it is within you. When you are seeking it from a relationship, you are missing the point. You are pushing it away. What you are attracting is not the divine definition of love, it is some other vibration. Perhaps it is one of your other definitions of love—lust, commitment, codependency, attention, fascination, partnership, addiction...resonance of some other sort.

What you seek is within you.

Where does love come from? It is when you recognize its real source that you start to give it freely. Many are operating from the illusion that love is limited. They believe it is hard to find. They believe it is rare. They believe it is outside of themselves. When you truly take a step back and observe your behavior, when you allow the beliefs underneath your actions to rise to the surface, you will start to see what your true beliefs about love itself are. What have you been taught? What have you taken on as the truth of love without questioning it? What has been modeled for you? Again, wipe the slate clean. This is liberation—a redefinition of the word itself, and from this, an opportunity to align with love joyfully and effortlessly.

CHAPTER 6

THE SOURCE
OF LOVE

Where does love come from? You are love. The Source of all, itself, is love, and you are an extension of this. And so, the source of love is always within you, as your natural state. Recognize where the "source" is—within you, not elsewhere. It is only in recognizing the love within you, in recognizing yourself as love, that you will be able to fully recognize this within others. This is where many of you become frustrated with your relationships and feel you do not understand love—but is it really love? For you to be able to discern love, to recognize love, you must first become familiar with the frequency. How do you become familiar with the frequency? You spend time in its vibration. You become familiar with it like an old friend, like a song you've heard on the radio a million times. When it plays, you know exactly what song it is, simply from the first few notes. A knowing.

Recognize that becoming familiar with this vibration is about sitting in the vibration itself as the most authentic version of you, as love. Simply allowing yourself to be aligned with Source itself, allowing this to move through you, and seeing this within yourself. And so, when you understand where it comes from, you understand it is not a limited resource. It is always within you, always available. You will not run out. And so, give it freely. Allow yourself to feel it deeply. Allow yourself to exchange it, to put more out into the world, knowing that your stores will never be emptied. It is an overflowing river, an endlessly filled cup.

Do you hold your breath because you fear you might run out of air? No, you let yourself be provided for. Because when you need a breath, you can always take it. And so it is with love—always an abundance available, an unlimited resource. Something that is always within you, that you can expand out into this world, reminding others of their own unlimited supply of love. When you fully embody this knowing—of where love is sourced, and that it is an unlimited resource—now you have the space and perspective to evaluate your interactions. When you choose to respond from anything other than love, where does this come from? Do you "save" your love, like saving your last few dollars for the perfect moment? This is where you are still in illusions, holding on so tightly out of fear of running out. Why is it that you hold yourself back from responding with love, from spreading it, from being generous with it? Allow it to amplify exponentially! What frequency are you choosing to radiate out? Do not forget that you are choosing.

From here you start to unravel your confused relationship with love, your projections onto love, where you are using it as an excuse to hide, where you are blaming it and judging it. Where you are afraid of it. Is it love itself you are afraid of? Or is it rejection, abandonment, betrayal? For some it is the former, for others the latter. This is where you must come to peace with free will and personal choice. You cannot control another. You can, however, shift energy in your favor. When you are living as love and giving it generously, that frequency is felt by those around you, and, if anything, would only support a positive shift in any interaction by bringing the truth to light.

Love dissolves illusions. It sheds light on that which is not showing up as love. But you cannot transmute fear, anger, resentment, guilt, or shame with more of the same. You are simply adding more to the energy of it. How do you want to contribute? How do you want to contribute to this world? How do you want to contribute to your relationships? What is the energetic environment you wish to create for yourself? When you respond from these lower frequencies, that is one way of adding more momentum to those vibrations within yourself. What is it you are looking to create? We return to the foundational frequency of the behavior—this is your responsibility. If you are looking to create a situation of love, this does not begin with guilt, shame, anger, or resentment. Be conscious of your intentions, of the energy that you are exchanging with those around you, and it will become clear to you how you are contributing to the collective and to your own life circumstances.

When you recognize there is an unlimited source of love, and you are an extension of that Source, you understand that you are love. This is your natural state. Where you have forgotten that within yourself is where you have forgotten who you really are. Where you are seeking love externally is where you are confused about the source of love itself. When you reconnect to Source as your source of love, living within you and through you, there is an unlimited supply.

CHAPTER 7

YOUR RELATIONSHIP WITH YOURSELF

And so, we must begin with you. We must begin with your relationship with yourself, with the frequency you emit, with how you choose to relate to others, and with how you see your relationships with others before we can fully understand the dynamics of those other relationships themselves. We must uncover where you are not fully in your authenticity. If you are not living as your authentic self, how could your relationships truly be aligned with unconditional love?

If you orient yourself from an understanding of energetic attraction, you understand that resonant frequencies find each other. That of a certain vibration is drawn to more of the same. When you put up a mask, when you project yourself to be someone different than who you really are, you are putting out a signal to attract more of that frequency, and you become entangled in relationships that are not truly a vibrational match. This can be felt in many ways.

Perhaps you feel as though the other person in the relationship does not truly see you for who you are. Perhaps you feel as though you can only reach a certain depth in conversation. Perhaps you feel stuck in one version of yourself—that you cannot grow or you will lose the relationship. Perhaps you feel a general disconnect—a deep knowing in your soul that you are settling in one way or another. Perhaps you feel like an outsider, like you won't fit in, like no one understands you. Perhaps you feel anxiety. Perhaps you feel like you are walking on eggshells. These feelings indicate dissonance within the system. This is not how divine love feels! Relationships aligned with love feel like flow. That is not to say you won't hit bumps in the river as you flow, but the underlying vibration is one of unconditional love. It is a safe container for you to be held. It is a safe container for you to be in as you hit those bumps, meet those challenges, and move through them into your next level of expansion.

Tune into the truth of your relationships. Are you all of yourself in these relationships? Do you feel seen as the true you? Do you feel safe to be all of you? Do you feel safe to expand, to grow, to shift, to change your mind? Or is there a piece of you that feels trapped in an older version of yourself? The truth is that not all relationships will be in your life forever, and this is not a bad thing. It is simply a part of the journey—meeting different people along the way, collecting beautiful experiences that teach you, prepare you, allow you to learn more about yourself, allow you to have different experiences. Some relationships are with you throughout the growth. Others are with you only for certain phases. It is part of the journey! How boring to stay in the same place the whole way through—that is not why you incarnated!

When you do not allow yourself to follow the flow, the changing rhythms in your life, the shifting seasons and relationships, you will feel an underlying dissonance—an underlying unhappiness or anxiety or perhaps disease in your body. This is your body's way of telling you things must change. This is your body's way of telling you that you are not fully learning the lessons and completing the contracts available to you. Your higher self, your true self within, is nudging you—listen! But it is up to you to do this—to listen to the truest version of yourself rather than the conditioning or the fear. To complete your contracts, you must listen to your intuition. The more you learn to listen to the true voice within, and follow that, your reality will recalibrate. The more you act in alignment with your intuition, with your true desires, with the truth of who you are, there is no other way for things to go than for your external reality, including your relationships, to recalibrate to be a vibrational match for your truth.

When you lie to yourself, when you pretend to be someone you're not, when you are caught up in what you "should" do rather than what you know is true for you—this is where you rob yourself of relationships that are truly a vibrational match for you. When you experience these relationships, ones that are truly a frequency match, you feel unconditional love. It is like two ingredients finding each other and making the most delicious recipe. It feels right. It has a beautiful, unique flavor, unlike anything else you've experienced before. You simply know it tastes delicious. Take either of those ingredients, and they can also pair beautifully with others. Each time, a different concoction is made, a different creation, a different flavor, a different energy. All serve their purpose. You can make chocolate salty or sweet! With the same ingredient, you can have a completely different experience each time.

There might be a period of your life when you crave salty snacks, and another when you crave sweet treats! This is your inner guidance knowing which vibration is most supportive for you right now in your current season. You need not question it or rationalize it. It is not that salty or sweet is right or wrong, better than or worse than. It's simply what you are called to at this time. But if you only allowed yourself to experience one flavor profile, you would always be left unsatisfied, you would always be craving more, you would feel hungry and not even know exactly what for. This is the beauty of expanding your range of experience and allowing yourself to taste different flavors, experience different frequencies, and collect this vibrational information for yourself, honoring what you require in that moment. Honoring what feels good to you. There might be some flavors that have aligned with your desires since childhood that will also stay with you through adulthood, and others that are only with you for a phase or a season. You might look quite fondly on that season, even if it feels far away! It is such with relationships—you are the ingredient.

You shift and change as well! What pairs nicely at one time, you might outgrow. It is from love to honor this process, allowing others to honor theirs as well. For if it is no longer a vibrational match for you, it is also misaligned for the other, but who will be the brave one to honor the shift first? Many of you sacrifice your happiness because you do not want to hurt others, but is it true love to stay in a dynamic that is not serving you? How would it feel for you to be on the other side of that? How would it feel to be in the dark that the other person in your relationship, whatever the dynamic, did not want to be there? That would not feel great for you either! And if it is no longer a vibrational match, then what else is waiting for you? Will you align with that?

Will you make space? When you do, you also allow the other to have space for what is truly a vibrational match to come to them, as well. Do you wish to block yourself or another from receiving that which is truly for their highest and best?

Settling is an energetic block that does not serve anyone. And so, it is love for everyone involved to allow this—releasing attachment to staying stuck, to staying the same, and opening the space for all to remain authentic to themselves, to live as the truest version of themselves, while understanding that what is true and authentic will shift and change, as this is the natural flow of the universe—movement. Staying stuck is what causes you to feel anxiety and misalignment, because it is resisting the natural flow of things. And so, allow the movement.

Tune into the feeling of when you can sense the pressure from another for you to stay the same. Can you feel this pressure? The stagnation? It is, quite literally, an energetic box. Tuning into that feeling, you know what would feel most loving would be to have open space and room to be free. This is the feeling of freedom you have been seeking. Understand that when you are free to dance and play and shift and change and grow, what is meant for you will of course still be there! It will find you. You need not force it. But where the box comes in, where the pressure comes from, is fear that it will not stay. It is a way of energetically shackling oneself to another, out of fear of loneliness. This is where you do not trust. This is where you fear the unknown. This is where you choose to create your own prison by blocking everyone involved from seeing and experiencing their truth. When you release the cords, the chains, the shackles, the expectations, and the boxes, and you allow all to flow in their authenticity, you see the truth. What unravels naturally is the truth of where energy is meant to be. What unravels is the truth of vibrational resonance. How willing are you to see the truth?

CHAPTER 8

SEEING THE TRUTH

You will start to understand more and more deeply how much of your behaviors and mindset around love and relationships are actually rooted in fear of truth. It is all illusion. And you wonder why you don't feel satisfied. You wonder why you seek more. Many blame their struggles with love on endless options. Is the problem really endless options, or is the problem the fear of really knowing and trusting yourself? It is not the existence of options, but your relationship to them. When you know yourself, when you know your truth, when you live your truth, when you live as the most authentic version of you, it does not matter how many options are available. You allow what is a match to flow to you. It is a natural, energetic filter. It is, in fact, when you get so used to choosing from the ego and the mind instead of the soul that you become overwhelmed with the options! But when you are choosing from your soul, it does not matter how many options there are. The right one will come straight to you. It will stand out to you. You will know within your body.

And so, to live authentically is to know the voice of your soul, to live as your highest self, to live as the truest you, to live from love, to choose from love for yourself and all others. And then, it is clear. In some ways, that takes "choice" out of it in the way many of you think about it. It is not so much about weighing pros and cons or worrying about being "wrong." There really is no "wrong." It is simply tuning into what is a vibrational match. When I am anchored into the frequency of love, where do I flow, and what flows to me? What am I drawn to? What am I excited about? What amplifies that frequency in me? What allows me to feel this frequency even more clearly? What is more of the same for me, uniquely? And so, you follow the flow.

When you are anchored in the vibration of love, which you will know more and more clearly the more you take time to tune in and connect directly with Source itself, illusions dissolve. When you are aligned with love, truth, and authenticity, you see clearly. You are no longer choosing or reacting or seeing from fear, anger, guilt, or conditioning. It is following your soul—the knowing that is within you—that sets you free. Notice where you are choosing from your mind or your ego. This is where you are choosing based on programming, previous conditioning, fear of what happened before, limiting beliefs, the piece of you that is operating from what you have known to be possible simply from your experience so far in this incarnation. But understand there are infinite other possibilities that you haven't experienced yet! Are you going to choose to continue to live from the conditioning and experiences you've already had, or step into the infinite possibilities of what could be? This is choosing your dreams. This is choosing what is more beautiful and wonderful than what you could have ever imagined. This is choosing creation, exploration, curiosity, and excitement. Allowing yourself to enter the infinite is choosing love. When you find yourself yearning for more, think—what if you allowed yourself to float in the infinite, the Source of all? There, you have found it!

If you wish to attract in truly aligned relationships, you must release the masks you are wearing. You must commit to living your truth and being the most authentic version of yourself, honoring that the whole way through. You must choose soul over ego and conditioning. You must allow yourself to be seen—the true you. You must allow yourself to see the true you, and from there it follows that you allow others to as well. You must choose to love you first. Consider it this way. What is from love—to tell your child to pretend to be someone they're not so other children will like them, or to encourage your child to express themselves authentically and allow others to see their innate divine magic? This is how they effortlessly attract their most aligned friends! Was it not simpler when you were a child? When did you let it become more complicated?

To be inauthentic, to choose anything other than to live your truth, is where you are in judgment of yourself. This is not from love. How can you truly know how to divinely love another, to experience that frequency in relationship, if you have not felt this within yourself? Again, you will attract what you are! You will attract more of the frequencies flowing within you! Anchor into divine love for yourself. When you commit to acting from love for yourself, in everything you do, you will notice that you attract in relationships with others of this same vibration.

What is it to act from love? Honoring your needs. Nourishing yourself. Fueling your body with nourishing, whole foods. Giving yourself rest and space when you need it. Prioritizing your joy. Following your inspiration and excitement. Releasing anything in your field that is draining your energy, making you sick, creating dis-ease in your system, and holding you back. Showing up for yourself. Keeping promises to yourself. Speaking positively to yourself. Reminding yourself how amazing you are. Making time for yourself. Living a life of joy rather than one of obligations and to-do's. Many of you don't even realize that you have created lives of to-do's, lives of living for other people, lives of putting yourself last. This is not treating yourself with love, so what do you expect to attract? Others who do the same. When you put yourself last and others first, you pretend this is love. You pretend this is for others, but it is serving no one. It is feeding a dynamic of codependency, of debt, of owing, of resentment, of guilt, of shame. It is coming from an energy of not choosing your truth, not choosing love.

We hope you do not misunderstand—this, of course, is not saying to not show up for others! In fact, when you are fully living as love, you will naturally desire to show up for others from a place of love, but this will not require sacrificing love for yourself in the process. Again, the key is the foundational frequency of the desire, of why you are doing what you're doing. Is it to get someone to like you? Is it to shift odds in your favor? Is it to manipulate someone's feelings? Is it to create an illusion of safety? Is it so someone owes you? Is it to avoid rejection or abandonment? Is it from a wounded place or a healed place? Is it actually for another, or is it for yourself? Is it to make yourself feel better temporarily instead of actually healing the wound? Giving from obligation is a very different experience than giving from divine love, without attachment. To be on the receiving end of giving from obligation is quite a different experience than receiving from someone who is truly giving from divine love without attachment. Where are there strings? Where are you creating strings?

Where are you tying yourself to others to source from outside yourself?

We invite you to reflect on relationships in a new way. Why is it that you feel inspired to enter into this relationship, of whatever sort? It is from this mindfulness you will start to notice where you are drawn to someone or something from a soul-led desire, from inspiration, from love, and where you are drawn to a dynamic or person from wounds, from fear, from jealousy, from ego, from the mind, from what makes sense, from what your ego thinks will get you ahead, from what will give you a false sense of safety. Many of you enter relationships seeking safety, trying to create safety, but it ends up creating the exact opposite effect. Allow relationships to form naturally based on resonance. To look for safety in a relationship by being anything other than your most authentic, truest self creates an illusion of a relationship, a relationship with a shaky foundation. This is the house of cards that falls apart.

What would it look like for you to take responsibility, where you can, of what you create? In any relationship, there are multiple energies coming together, and you are a piece of this! You can set the frequency of the relationship. To create a relationship consciously is to orient yourself from love. Be intentional with what you are looking to create in the dynamic. Be intentional with your why. Be clear with your intentions. What is it you wish to build? What is the frequency you wish to embed within the dynamic? Build from the same frequency you wish to be in—you will not land in a different vibrational place. When you are clear in your intentions to build from love, from truth, from authenticity, from true love for yourself and another, you act in alignment with this, and what previously looked like "choosing" now becomes simply following the flow. It is effortless to know your truth. The resistance to acting upon it is from the limitations of the mind and the ego.

CHAPTER 9

ASKING FOR MORE AND CHOOSING LOVE

Do you dare to dream bigger? Do you dare to ask for more? Are you afraid to ask for the divine love that you deserve? Where are you choosing to settle? Again, it is key to be honest with yourself. The way so many of you keep yourselves stuck, the way so many of you keep yourselves in the energies of yearning and longing rather than having right now, rather than creating the reality you desire, is choosing to settle. You are afraid to change. You are afraid to ask for what you really want, from a soul-aligned place. Wanting from the ego is quite different from desiring from the soul. Where does this come from? There has been much conditioning about being greedy. "Don't ask too much. Don't be too much." You have been programmed to believe you are full of yourself if you dream bigger or dare to ask for more. Your mind says, who are you to ask for more?

It is key to first become aware of the foundational frequency of the desire. Is the "want" for more from a place of ego or the mind, or is it from your soul? Is it aligned with love? Where you tell yourself you are not worthy of desiring divine love is where you are disconnected from Source. This is where you are disconnected from yourself as an extension of Source. This is where you have forgotten who you are. This is where you are in illusions about where love comes from, and about what is available to all. This is where you are stuck in a scarcity mindset, allowing fear and scarcity to run the show. If you wish to live in the limitations you create for yourself, then this is your choice. But understand it is not greedy to ask for that which you are. It is not greedy to ask for your soul's desire, to claim it, and to align with it. This is the natural state of things. The calling is within you for a reason. It is guiding you to your truth. Your truth is love.

There is nothing you need to do to earn love. It is your birthright. It is your natural state. This is where you start to deprogram what it means to love and to be loved. Did you learn you had to be "perfect," you had to be "right," you had to be different, or you had to do something to earn love? This is not our definition of love, but rather conditional "love" that you call it, which is really allowance in a field rather than love itself. Is that truly love? To set parameters on another, to tell them to live in fear, to be anything other than their authentic selves, and only then will there be "love"—this is not love. This is an attempt to control. This is fear. Some of this is intentional, and much of it is not, because the programs run so deep. But it is you who is here to break the status quo. It is you who is ready to be the living example of what it looks like to live from love and to relate with love—the true definition. It is you who is here to be a living example of love that shines so bright, it invites others to start to question their own definitions, and why they are settling. It is quite plain to us—where you settle is where you betray yourself. Where you settle is where you rob others of the opportunity to find their perfect, most aligned matches as well. To be with your most aligned matches is the natural state of things. Love is your birthright. There is nothing else you need to do to earn it. You do not need to be different from who you truly are. Can you allow yourself to be divinely loved?

Here we come to receiving, for this is where the blocks lie. Are you fully open to receiving love? Many of you are not fully open to receiving love as you have understood it previously, and are also blocking yourselves from fully receiving divine love. Others are blocked from receiving love as defined by those around them, which is really obligation, because there is an inherent knowing that it is not truly love, although it may not be recognized as such. And so, where are you making yourself wrong? Where are you telling yourself you're too greedy? Where are you telling yourself you will be hurt, or betrayed, or abandoned? Where are you desiring something but keeping the door closed so you can't receive it? To receive, you must open your heart. It is to live with an open heart.

You must also be ready for the truth to be revealed, for love is truth. The same way that many hide from the potent frequency of truth, many hide from the potent frequency of divine love—because it transforms, because it transmutes, because it is a force, because it shines light on all that is not authentic, on all that is out of alignment with love. You are afraid to be hurt, and we understand this. But how much of this is a projection? How much of this is expecting what happened before to happen again? What if instead, you recognized that what happened before was a learning lesson that offered opportunities for energetic shifts so that what happened before need not happen again, if you fully integrate the lesson? It is all preparing you. Claim what you desire. Claim who you are. Live as love, and allow yourself to receive this. Where this is most important is from yourself.

You will see where you are blocked from divine love when you explore your relationship with yourself, how you take care of yourself, and how you talk to yourself. Many of you hope that this will change when you are in a relationship with another, so you seek love with another person, all the while not loving yourself. And so, you are outsourcing your love, which is a recipe for unhappiness. This is dependency. If you depend on another for your happiness, to feel love, to receive love, then you are giving your power away. You are giving them control of your happiness, rather than choosing it for yourself. It is your choice, and that is powerful. You get to always choose your happiness. You get to choose to live, to be, to receive divine love. Will you choose this? To choose this is not to depend on another for love or happiness, as it is not your responsibility to provide this for another either. It is to enter into a relationship remembering how whole you are, sourcing from Source itself, knowing that love is unlimited, and from here you can see clearly. From here, you need not depend on another for what is already within you.

CHAPTER 10

MIRRORING

That being said, part of the human experience is learning more about yourself through your relationships with others, for there is always something to learn from every connection, understanding that all are connected, and all are living out different aspects of the human experience to contribute to the collective consciousness. Through each connection, you are able to see different parts of yourself. Think of it as seeing more angles in the physical. Will you see more with no mirrors, with one, with three, or with fifty?

Certain interactions will reveal things to you that you have not yet uncovered about yourself—perhaps things you have been hiding, ways of showing up you did not realize were not serving you, ways that you were living from your mind, your ego, or your conditioning instead of from your soul, ways that you were unintentionally living from fear instead of love. In other interactions, you might find you are deeply reminded of your essence as love. Certain interactions might help you remember your beauty, your grace, your power, how truly amazing you are—seeing this reflection. But it is different to be reminded, to allow yourself to be supported in the remembrance, than it is to source from another.

The difference is truly the same as fishing for someone else, or teaching them to fish themselves. Which is more helpful? What a beautiful gift, to be reminded of your own inherent beauty, worthiness, and essence as love! But let's not misunderstand that reminder as a place to source from. It is not that person who is giving you those things. It is them reflecting what is within you back to you. This is already sourced within you, and they are reflecting that energy. And so, when you feel what you perceive to be love in your dynamic with another, recognize where you are perceiving it as the other being your source of love, as the energy coming from them to you. Simply reflect on that for a moment.

First, this reflects a knowing that there is love within that other. You are feeling that frequency. Can you see how that is Source moving through them? The same Source moving through you? Is it only what moves through them, or what the dynamic brings out in you? Do you see the difference? You can perceive it as coming from them, or you can perceive the mixture of frequencies to unlock, to activate, to call upon that which is already within you, because the emotion is within you. When you feel the emotion, even if it is that of another, it is within you. And so, the vibration is within you. What if you perceived the love you feel not as theirs flowing into you, as your source, but rather as one tuning fork activated and the other matching its frequency? The sound comes from both tuning forks, individually. The frequency from the first activates the same frequency in the second.

Do you give love, or do you share it? Do you give love, or do you express it? When you give it, do you feel depleted? If so, is this divine love, when you remember that there is an unlimited source? This depletion is telling you something else. You might reflect upon that which gives you energy and that which drains your energy. We prefer to think of it as shifting the vibration rather than getting rid of it, to help you understand the energy is not gone—for everything is energy, but it is shifting form. And so, you might feel the tone get lower or higher. The color might get brighter or duller. What dims you, and what brightens you? It is vital you understand that divine love is within you, and no one can take this from you, the same way that you are not taking it from another. It is illuminating what is already within you.

We offer this shift in perception for you to relate in a more liberated way, rather than looking to others to find something that is already within you. From here, you might approach relationships with curiosity in terms of, *what frequency is this matching and activating within me?* As you feel the frequency of your relationship with another, get curious about what is brought out. The mixture of another's energy, or frequency, and your own will highlight a certain vibration within you, and this helps you see more of the most authentic version of yourself, another side of your authenticity, another angle to look at.

We will address that yes, you can feel others' emotions in your body. But is it really theirs, or, again, the resonant frequency within yourself that is being brought up within you? This is similar to how when you put a glass of water next to another, the information stored in the water is transferred from one glass to another. This is similar to how one tuning fork plays the same tone as another when they are placed side by side. Without touching, the information is transferred. And so, it is all in perception to recognize where it is coming from. It is recalibrating the energy within rather than sourcing from without. If you understood that you were not getting energy from another but rather observing a frequency, would you relate differently?

What happens so often is that the vibrations get muddled. You forget where you are sourcing from. You confuse what is you with what is another. You think that because it is in relation to another that it is from them, and you have a sense of "losing" yourself. You have not lost yourself—we will remind you of this! But what we will also remind you of is the importance of anchoring into your own energy, into your own frame, and first coming from a clear foundation of knowing yourself. This is why the groundwork of self-love, of knowing yourself, of exploring yourself, of learning your beauty and your gifts and your desires, but also your fears and your wounds and worries, is all so important—to see all of this, to love all of this, and to know yourself above all else. This is how you do not "get lost," as you call it, in the relationship—you first understand yourself. If you were to enter a dark forest, would you not first turn on a flashlight?

Learning the voice of your soul, learning the voice of love, and living from this is the foundation. That is what must be done first in order to relate clearly and, while holding your own vibration, to relate from an empowered place. That step is the same as turning on the flashlight before entering the forest—it allows you to see clearly. It is so you can see what is around you, observe it, and decide which direction you want to go in. It is to act from love for yourself. Where you throw yourself in the dark without your own light is where you feel like you are lost. Are you really lost, or are you just not seeing what is there? Turn on the light.

Find clarity within yourself first. Learn yourself. Love yourself. When you understand why you are the way you are, and when you get to know yourself better than anyone else, you can communicate clearly.

You can take responsibility for your own energy, your behavior, your choices. You will have deeper compassion for others when you live with compassion for yourself. How can another truly know you if you do not know yourself? Are you depending on others to get to know you for you? Are you depending on others to pull out the things you must know, rather than exploring them personally first? Are you depending on others to pull things out for you, and put it together for you, or are you willing to observe and learn from those connections for yourself? Notice where you are dependent on others.

CHAPTER 11

THE KEY TO LOVING

Again, there will be many things that come to light within the relationship dynamic, but to depend on this alone, to depend on someone else pointing out those things to you, in order to get to know yourself is like hitchhiking instead of driving your own car. It's your choice if you wish to wait for that ride and limit your range of experience when it comes to where you could go. Getting to know yourself is loving yourself. Do you want to know all of whom you love? To be anchored into love is to see all from truth, clearly—nothing needs to be left in the dark! And so it is not only with love for yourself, but love for others. What a gift to enter any sort of relationship with the self-awareness of who you are! When you do, you will be clearer in your communication about your needs and desires. You will be clearer with your intentions. You will take responsibility for your actions and emotions. You will be able to express the roadmap for how to love you.

Many of the issues that arise in relationships are because of miscommunication about needs and desires. Learn how you want to be loved—how you feel an expression of love—and now you can clearly express that to another. But if you do not know how you desire to be loved, how you best feel, understand, and receive love, or what feels good to you, then how can you expect another to figure it out? Where are you expecting someone else to figure out something that is your responsibility to know?

And we will be clear, you learn this about yourself through relationships! Through relating with others and having different experiences, you notice your feelings. You notice what feels good, what feels resonant. You collect this information about yourself, and you are able to use that information to communicate. You keep refining the "experiment" through the information you collect about yourself, and this allows the experience to become more loving, more illuminating, and more liberating. You experience things, you recognize how it feels, and you learn more about yourself. It is communicating what you have learned about yourself—what feels good, what you desire, what you need—that allows you to see the truth of the vibrational resonance of the relationship. It is this truth that allows you to emit a clear vibrational signal about what you desire and what you are available for. This is how you attract and create your most aligned relationships.

This is what happens often in relationships—people enter the relationship not knowing what they really desire in terms of how love is expressed clearly to them, and then they are upset when the other person does not express love in the way they want. What is that way? Do you know? Have you expressed it clearly? Love is expressed in many ways. The irritation is not really about that person not loving you the "right" way, because there is not necessarily a "right" way, but the issue is in communication. You cannot communicate clearly if you do not know what needs to be communicated. Learn how you receive love. What makes you feel loved? How do you express love? Give the person you love the roadmap, because they want to love you! What a beautiful gift! It's the difference between giving them the one correct key and giving them a ring of ten keys, tapping your foot in annoyance as they try each one in the door. Where are you expecting others to know that which you have not communicated? Where are you expecting others to figure out for you that which you are too afraid to figure out or admit to yourself?

There is resistance to this for many, because they make themselves wrong or tell themselves they're too much for expressing their needs or their desires. They would rather the other figure it out first while they pretend to be unaware, as a way of abdicating responsibility for speaking up about what they need. This is another iteration of people-pleasing tendencies. This is another iteration of being afraid to be fully seen. This is another iteration of hiding one's authentic expression. They tell themselves, *however that person wants to express their love, I will adjust to it.* When you love another, doesn't it make you feel good to know exactly how to make your feelings clear to that person so they can fully receive your love? This is how you feel connected and on the same page, because you are speaking the same language. There are no breakdowns in communication. This is also how you quickly and easily see the truth of how the relationship can flow, and if it is an aligned match. If someone is not willing to or does not desire to speak your language in terms of love and connection, would you truly rather not know? Part of loving is understanding yourself and the other—what are our desires? How do we express and give love? This is a gift, because it is the key. Clear communication is love. Both parties will feel frustrated when you are searching in the dark when someone could just turn on the light.

Why is it that you are afraid to fully receive? It is this fear, often based on expecting previous experiences to happen again, that creates the pattern of subconsciously choosing those who cannot give you exactly what you need. This creates a self-fulfilling prophecy, or a situation where you unintentionally settle because you are afraid of your heart breaking once more. But in the situation you are looking to avoid, was the frequency of that relationship truly love, or something else to begin with? We will remind you that when your heart breaks, it is given an opportunity to grow stronger, to love more deeply, and to feel more deeply. It is this depth of love that is such a gift. That is what you are here to experience—the full range of emotions, all useful, all giving helpful information. Flowing in the sea of emotions that you can access in this form is perhaps the most beautiful part of the journey.

Without these emotions, how would you feel throughout your day? Can you imagine looking at a beautiful sunset and feeling nothing? These deep, rich feelings create your experience. It is the contrast of these emotions that allows you to experience the highs, the love, the peace, the joy, the gratitude, and the excitement, which you appreciate even more deeply when you have felt the opposite. And so, when you block yourself from receiving, you block yourself from your desires, and you wonder why you are unsatisfied and unfulfilled. You complain about the people you are attracting into your life, but you must remember that who and what you attract is based on your vibration and your choices.

Where are you continuing to allow relationships in your life that are not meeting you with love? Where are you continuing to share space and enabling the interactions to continue? Where are you complaining about those relationships, but also feeding the current energy of the relationship instead of showing up at a new frequency to create space for an energetic shift overall? We understand that this might strike a chord with many, but it is quite simple when you take a step back and look at the decisions you are making in your life and what you are saying yes to. Understand that this is all vibrational information for the universe, updated signals of what you are allowing, what you want, what frequency you are welcoming in. What choices have you yet to take responsibility for? Where are you still blaming others?

CHAPTER 12

RECEIVING LOVE

Some of you resist receiving because you believe you are not good enough or not worthy. Some of you resist receiving because you have been told that you must do something to earn or receive love. Some of you resist receiving because you are afraid of your own depth of emotion. Get to the root of the fear. What would it look like in your life for you to receive a bit more? To allow yourself to receive more love? So many of you enter a relationship and let yourself walk only to the edge of the pool instead of diving in and enjoying it while it's there. Many of you do not make the most of the opportunities in front of you. Many are afraid to go fully into a situation because, what if it ends? What if it does?

If it's going to end either way, you might as well dive into the experience! Otherwise, you end up living your whole life halfway in and halfway out, never letting yourself fully love or be loved, limiting how much you feel. When you do this, you always look for more. It's a feeling you can't shake. What is that? Your intuition is guiding you to go fully in. If it's not this, there's something better. You open yourself up to what is truly for your highest and best when you go fully into the experience to see the truth of what is and what could be, and then take action based on the frequency you wish to maintain or activate in your life. Whether the relationship or experience is one day, one week, one month, one year, one decade— is it not all worth receiving?

Receive each moment of life fully, each experience fully, and watch as you expand. Watch as you live your purpose, as you reignite the spark of inspiration in your life every day. Life is not magical just because of grandiose moments that come once in a blue moon. It is magical because you have the ability to be fully present to the magic and receive the magic available in every moment. You can either choose to perceive it, or choose to move through it unconsciously. You can watch a film with full presence, allowing yourself to move through the storyline with the characters, allowing yourself to learn about yourself and the world around you through the story, allowing yourself to be moved to tears of sadness or laughter, feeling a complete, deeply moving experience by the time it is over. You can also watch the same film barely paying attention, and when it ends you might feel bored, or unmoved, or like it was a waste of time. You simply were not present to the experience, so what do you expect? Meet your present moment with awareness.

From this, we invite you to meet others consciously. We give this reminder often because it is so key. When you understand how vibrational attraction works, when you understand that there are no coincidences, when you commit to working with the universe and becoming present to the magic that is always available, you will shift your energy to be open to others coming in. Source works through people. Opportunities are always available, and you never know who will lead you there! You never know who might walk into your life and entirely shift it, whether you experience their company for ten minutes, a few weeks, a few years, or an entire lifetime. Are you allowing yourself to be pleasantly surprised? When you are hoping to align with expansive relationships, are you truly open to whoever comes into your field?

The way we have seen much of your society progress is that many move through life unaware. You do not talk to "strangers." You call them strange because you don't already know them. Well, how do you think you will get to know them? When someone is ready to come into your life, they will, but are you ready? Are you open? Notice where you want something different, yet you are not open to something different. Notice where you want something different, but you keep saying yes to what's familiar. You keep saying yes to different versions of what you've already experienced before. Notice where you fear what is new. What if the resonance of what's new makes it quite obvious that it is time to release what is more familiar?

Do you notice what is right in front of you? And this is a key point, for it touches on the root of why so many are continuously yearning for more—you are not recognizing what is right in front of you. When you are present, conscious, and living in unconditional love, you are able to see the beauty in all experiences and in all people. Challenge yourself to open up to seeing the beauty in all people— the different ways of thinking, the different ways of exploring, the different interests, the different personalities. What a beautiful range, all able to teach you something and help you unlock new parts of yourself!

It is often the people you don't see coming that shift your life in profound ways. If you wish for the energy in your life to shift quickly, if you wish for changes to be made quickly, if you wish for a quantum leap, be open to who drops in your path. Your entire life could shift in an instant from a serendipitous, divinely designed meeting! What have you been asking for? Might it be delivered through someone? Perhaps this is someone you've known for quite some time, but a new perception is available. Perhaps it is someone who is new in your sphere. But are you open to receiving them? Or are you expecting your life to change without anything actually changing?

Remember that energy shifts in many ways, and feelings, which are energy, shift quite often as well. This makes some of you feel uneasy—what if someone's feelings shift overnight? For others, this is liberating—you never know whose role in your life is going to rapidly shift overnight! Is your life partner right in front of your eyes? Is your most aligned best friend someone right in front of you, someone you have been overlooking all along? Energy will shift form as it is meant to, as is directed, as is resonant. This is where you have the opportunity to master the art of detachment.

How attached are you to things staying the same? This is against the flow of nature. How attached are you to someone else staying a certain way, or playing a certain role for you? This is not unconditional love. And how would this feel for you, if another so desperately wanted you to be someone else? If someone else decided for you who your authentic self is, for their own false sense of safety, their own comfort, their own wants, their own convenience? This is where you do not trust. This is where you are operating from fear. This is where you are out of alignment with unconditional love. Where are you in your own way of it working out better than you could have ever imagined? Where are you limiting what is available to you, because you are choosing potential possibilities based on what your mind knows, what is in your reality right now, and what you can understand, but neglecting the infinite other opportunities and possibilities that are also available to you? There are so many other possibilities that want to reveal themselves to you!

CHAPTER 13

FOLLOWING YOUR INTUITION

Living an expanded, abundant life is your birthright, but this will require you to stop limiting yourself by operating primarily from your mind and ego. Allow your soul to lead you directly to the path of highest alignment and expansion. What a joy to be pleasantly delighted as you encounter different people, experiences, and energies on your path! And so, dedication to living this kind of life is dedication to your intuition. Pay attention to what is coming up in your reality—the themes, the people, the feelings. When your emotions are suddenly drawing you toward something or someone you didn't expect, this is your next step. It is key to tune into this question—is it your emotions, or your mind? We will speak more on attraction later. But when you are intuitively drawn to a person or a place or a thing, this is the next step on the path to vibrationally aligned relationships.

Perhaps the relationship you seek, of whatever sort, will begin in a location you never expected. Perhaps the relationship you seek comes through an opportunity from someone you never expected. Perhaps the relationship is not with them, but with their friend or their acquaintance. Perhaps you are drawn to someone who suggests an event at which you meet another person who is dear friends with the person you have been seeking. Allow your soul to do its magic. Honor its infinite wisdom. It is not outside of you. It is within you. When you drop into the flow, when you follow your intuition, when you work with the universe instead of resisting it, you are constantly in a state of calibrating to vibrationally aligned relationships, without even trying. This is the natural state of things—what is a vibrational match comes to you when you are open to receiving it. But you must notice the resistance that exists. Who in your life is no longer a match?

As you continue on your journey, as you learn more about yourself, as you explore new pieces of yourself, as more desires become unlocked, your vibration shifts. It only makes sense that there will be people and things in your reality that are no longer a match, as you have shifted. Sometimes they shift with you, but sometimes not. And so, you consistently take stock of the relationships and experiences in your life. Is this still aligned with who I really am, now? Or was it a beautiful season, but no longer calibrated to the authentic me? When you are clogging up your field with things that are no longer a vibrational match, there is no room for the energy to move. There is no room for what is a match for you to flow to you. And so, it is crucial that you continue to honor what feels good and what does not. This goes beyond your mind.

Many of you hold onto relationships that are no longer serving you because your mind gets in the way. You try to rationalize your emotions when they are not meant to be rationalized. There is a time for the mind, for thought, and for logic, and there is also a time for emotion. What if your emotions were the trigger point for your infinite wisdom to come through, instead of trying to force your emotions from the place of your mind? This is where you limit yourself—when you are trying to control them, when you are not listening to their wisdom, when you are justifying your actions from a place of logic rather than listening to your soul, which is speaking to you through your emotions and through your inner knowing. It is not that you do not know what your soul is saying—you simply must tune into its language.

Understand that your mind and your soul speak different languages, and you can be an expert in both! But you will always find yourself stuck if you continue to choose your relationships based on your mind's thoughts and logic. This is choosing a path of limitation. This is choosing settling—there, we said it! Let your soul lead you to what is greater than you could have ever imagined. When you try to rationalize what you are feeling, what you know on a soul level, where you are guided—where does this come from? Why is it that you are trying to make sense of it? This is where you don't trust yourself. This is where you are still operating from programming and conditioning–that you have to know why, that you have to explain why, that the knowing has to come from a logical starting point, that it has to make sense to other people. This makes sense if you are explaining a math equation, but divine wisdom—your soul knowing—doesn't have a logical place from which it "starts." It simply drops in, and you listen. It is a shortcut. It is the quick way. It is accessing the infinite source of wisdom available to all. It is much faster than your logical brain, and so, you can choose your timeline.

CHAPTER 14

COMPLETING RELATIONSHIP CONTRACTS

You can choose whether you stay in relationships or not. When you choose to stay in relationships that do not serve you, you will feel the vibrational pull. You will feel the dissonance within yourself, the dis-ease. You also clog up energetic space for that other person, in addition to yourself. That space could be taken up by someone who is truly expansive for both parties. What is for the highest and best for you, genuinely, truly, is also for the highest and best for all, even if adjusting the situation feels difficult at first. Even if it is emotional. Is this a bad thing—that you care? That you honor the relationship? We think it's a beautiful thing. What would it look like to celebrate the chapter, to send gratitude, to be so grateful for the experience? What would it look like to close or transmute the relationship with love?

We would like to touch on this—is it required to completely close the relationship? First, nothing is required of you. You get to choose how you navigate your relationships. But we will offer a perspective. Is it energetically helpful to completely close the relationship? From our perspective, it depends on the circumstances, and this is something you know within yourself. We will say, the "closure" is more energetic than anything else. We understand some people resonate more with the word "transition" than "ending" or "closing." But we will also say, many of you make it harder on yourselves because you believe it must be a big dramatic ending, cutting someone off for life, rather than simply an energetic shift. Where the conversation must be had is when it is required for the energetic closure to truly occur. When that happens, it is a part of your highest growth experience to speak your truth and act from an authentic place. If you are not speaking up or being clear from a place of fear or avoidance, this is something to look at.

The answer comes when you align with love—what is the loving way to move forward on both ends? Not all things need to be said verbally, but sometimes they do. Remember, these relationship dynamics are opportunities for you to learn about yourself and to live as the most empowered version of yourself. If you tune into your decisions and notice them coming from fear or avoidance, that is something to pay attention to! When you avoid the conversation from a place of fear or avoidance, the energy is still open. The contract is not yet complete. The cord is still there. And so, the answer comes from honesty. When you align with divine honesty within yourself, you don't need to ask others what to do—you simply know. It will depend on the situation.

What if it was not bad or wrong to feel sadness or grief when a relationship shifts? What if it didn't necessarily mean you made the wrong decision? Why have you decided this is wrong, rather than simply letting your emotions flow through? It is more than okay for different emotions to flow through you as a relationship dynamic changes! This is how you release any frequencies that might have been hidden within. This is simply the flow of energy, and you can allow it to be so. But you will notice where you are so afraid of your emotions! Notice where you avoid fear. As you resist it, you actually add more energy to it. As you resist it, as you sweep it under the rug, it builds and builds and turns into something bigger. What if you looked at it with love? What if you felt it and gave it space to move through. Your emotions are simply frequencies. Some days it rains, and other days the sun shines. Is the rain bad? Does the rain want to hurt you? The rain provides water for your plants. The rain is part of the cycles of nature, the seasons that change, the energetic balance of the earth. It simply is. Can you find beauty in the whole range of experience? In all seasons and cycles?

Taking responsibility for your reality means being aware of what is in your energetic field. What is supporting you in who you want to be, and what is not? If someone is not, this does not make them bad or wrong, it simply means it is not fully aligned for you at this phase, and you might choose to reallocate your energetic resources—your time and space. Notice what stories you create around this. What do you tell yourself it means?

CHAPTER 15

SOUL-RESONANT FRIENDSHIPS

It is from this place that we will touch on family and friendships, and the "love" many of you think you feel in these dynamics. We ask you to receive this perspective with an open mind and open heart. Perhaps this is the permission you need to follow your intuition. Perhaps this is the nudge you need to live your truth. Perhaps this is the reminder you need to appreciate certain relationships more deeply. Perhaps this is the reflection point you have been waiting for. And if it does not resonate, then it does not. But we will add that the points of this text that trigger you the most are, in fact, the most important places to look in terms of restructuring the way your society functions so it is in alignment with divine love.

To create a different reality for the collective, to create this new earth you speak of, is a co-creation. It will require relating differently, and that will require looking at the most deeply ingrained expectations in society and acknowledging where they are no longer serving you as a collective. Be brave enough to explore the places you most desperately want to keep in the dark, for there is a reason why you resist looking there. What you avoid and what you fear will not go away or get any better when you push it into a corner. The only way to work out the energetic knot is to massage it.

We will start with friendships. How have so many of these formed? Before you really understand yourself, these often form based on surface-level commonalities like where you live, who you are friends with, and hobbies. But as you explore your own depths and your own truths, you might notice that under the surface, there isn't resonance. How many of you are hanging onto friendships out of convenience? They are simply around and always have been. How many of you are holding onto friendships because they are comfortable? They know you (or at least, a version of you), they're easy (because they're already there), and it makes sense. The most incredible relationships often do not make sense. Friendships based on soul resonance are what you are yearning for.

As you emit your frequency more clearly, it becomes easier for you to attract others who are of a similar frequency. This is what you call soul family—those who you choose to incarnate with as a group, and eventually find each other. Through these connections, you reactivate to new levels of expansion and growth. This is different from comfortability in relationships. When you evaluate your relationships, ask, *does this person truly see me? Am I my most authentic self in this relationship?* Remember that just because something is comfortable does not necessarily mean it is also expansive and supportive on your journey of embodying your most fully expressed self.

The most beautiful relationships will help you feel comfortable in the discomfort. You will feel held and seen in the new explorations, the shifts, and the growth. The limiting relationships will be so comfortable, you are afraid to stretch out. Long-term, that comfort becomes uncomfortable because your natural state is growth, expansion, and movement. And so, there are different types of "comfort." You will notice this in how you feel when you first meet someone. Your ability to discern soul resonance will depend on how much you know the voice of your soul, how much you know yourself, and the frequency you are vibrating at, at that time.

And so, many perceive certain relationships as soul-aligned when really they are just a vibrational match for what they are used to, which is not necessarily what is for their highest and best. Notice where the vibrational match is to what you are already comfortable with, or to what you have experienced before. This is why people continue to choose different versions of the same vibration—they feel it, they know it, and because they are comfortable with what they know, they choose it. But when you have truly shifted your frequency, if you are truly looking for a different type of relationship, coming in contact with that will feel different because it is a different frequency. It will feel expansive. It will stretch you. It might even "trigger" you at first, because it's unfamiliar! Again, we invite you to evaluate what different relationships bring out in you.

If you find that in a certain relationship you do not like what is brought out in you, then it is up to you to show up as the most authentic you. You do not need to figure it all out. You can simply choose to act as the most authentic version of yourself, and the truth will be revealed. When you act as the most authentic version of yourself, this gives others the room to recalibrate to this. It welcomes them in. You might be surprised how many people are excited to support you in being all of you! Because they love you! But you might also recognize that certain relationships don't seem to "work" anymore when you are the most "you" you can be. So the question becomes, do you stay stuck in illusions to appease someone else, or do you honor yourself? When you align yourself with divine love, the answer is clear.

CHAPTER 16

THE ILLUSION OF OBLIGATION

You are not obligated to anyone. No one is obligated to you. This will be the most prominent shift in your society—when you stop acting from obligation. That is not to say you won't or can't or shouldn't choose to show up for or support others in whatever way, but there is a difference between doing something because you desire to—because you choose to—and because you are obligated to. Let your actions come from desire, not obligation.

Structures and expectations rooted in obligation come from scarcity and fear. Start to pay attention to how much of the language and messaging in your society come from a place of obligation—of owing, of expectation, of "this is how it is." "I'm your friend." "I'm your family." And what is that meant to mean? What is the energy underneath that? It is a reminder of an expectation that someone else is trying to force upon you, but it is up to you to hold the higher frequency of unconditional love. When someone is reminding you of this expectation, it is an attempt at control, even if this is not their conscious intention. Underneath is the frequency of, "This is the expectation. This is the rule, and we obey the rules." Why is that the rule? Not all rules are good ones. Are guidelines not meant to be updated? Does a label require a lifetime commitment? Commitments don't have to last forever. And so, we consider a fair response to be to explore the definition of "friend" itself. From there, you can ask, is this how a friend shows up?

Our perspective on this obligation energy is that it is outdated and no longer a vibrational match for your society and where you are headed—what you are ready to step into. It is not a vibrational match for the reality you are looking to create for the collective. And so, you must make choices in alignment with the reality you wish to live in. A different reality will require different choices. A different timeline will require different choices. As you make this shift, you will notice that some people are choosing based on their current reality and what would align with staying in it, and others are making different choices that are calibrated to the new reality, and so their relationships and entire world are completely different. Living in two different realities on seemingly the same plane. This will be part of the process. Many of you will choose to relate in the "new" way, really the natural way, from a soul-aligned place, from divine love, while others will still be in the process of relating from fear, obligation, and ego. The vibrational difference in relationships will be distinct.

Where does this obligation come from? We will call it primitive. You could argue that everything serves you in some way, but which version of you is it serving? And so, when you do not have access to resources, it might be vital for a tight-knit group to stay together, to protect each other, to honor each other. In this scenario, perhaps obligation energy was supportive for survival, which was really from fear of not having enough or not being safe. We will offer that the energy of commitment would be more aligned with unconditional love than obligation, to create a similar effect. But when the previously mentioned example is not the circumstance, does obligation energy serve you? This is what we will untangle next—family.

CHAPTER 17

FAMILY
DYNAMICS

Over time, a belief has been threaded throughout the collective consciousness of your society that because someone is part of your biological family, there is an obligation to deal with whatever their behavior or desires might be. This has enabled people to stay in unhealthy dynamics and been used as justification for acting out of alignment with unconditional love. This is also where many have abdicated responsibility for upholding unconditional love for themselves and others. When you are in alignment with love for yourself, the way you treat others shifts drastically. There are some people who feel a sense of infallibility, a sense of protection, because of the norms of "family" dynamics. They act from a belief that they need not take full responsibility for themselves, and they expect "family" to always stay by their side. On the other side of this, others feel guilty or shameful if they remove themselves from unhealthy dynamics.

To stay in a dynamic because of guilt or shame only feeds more of the same. This feeds dis-ease and sickness within the unit as a whole. This is another angle to the wounds, traumas, and dis-ease that is passed down through family lines. It is vibrational, and it can be passed down between generations. Part of transmuting this is choosing differently. You can shift the vibrational coding. Where do you have different expectations for friends, lovers, and family? We invite you to explore why this is so. Who do you lower or adjust your standards for, and why? The energy of guilt is threaded deeply within family units, along with shame and fear—fear of being cast out, fear of being abandoned, fear of not being provided for. Quite simply, that is not the frequency of love.

There is a new definition of family available to you—a new way of relating to family that is available to you. We invite you to tune into what that means and define it for yourself first. It is no coincidence that you chose the family you did. You chose this on a soul level before you incarnated. Why might you have chosen it? There are lessons to learn from everyone, in all dynamics. Your soul did not necessarily choose your family for you to stay entangled. No matter how it plays out, the opportunity is and has been to uphold the vibration of love. The contract was not necessarily to continue previously ingrained dynamics, but to offer an opportunity for expansion and healing.

Showing up differently is the path to healing for many. There is healing for all when you show up with unconditional love for all. Acting from that frequency means acting from love for yourself—in the situations you allow yourself to be in, in being responsible for your field, in what energetic dynamics you engage in. If it is unhealthy, it is unhealthy, and it is from love for yourself that you step out of or change the dynamic, being the example of upholding love for yourself. It is also love for the other—by maintaining the frequency of divine love, this offers others the opportunity to calibrate there as well. When they are acting from anger, resentment, guilt, or shame, this is not the truth of who they are! But when there is no perceived resistance, when there is no awareness of dissonance, the energy often stays the same.

What is the real fear beneath acting from full love for yourself? Is it that you do not want to upset your parents? Your siblings? It is not your responsibility to manage their emotions. You cannot control their reactions or emotions. We will play with the perspective a bit. Perhaps you do not want to step out of a dynamic because you do not want to upset someone in your family. Perhaps this is obligation energy, fear, guilt, automatic processing, or conditioning. If you are all worried about not upsetting each other when it comes to family, how would their behavior make sense in that paradigm? Are they worried about the same?

Sometimes healing means stepping away in order to eventually step back in. If you are unhappy in your family dynamic, that will not change until you make different choices. This could be choosing to relate differently, choosing to show up differently, or choosing to communicate differently—always starting with yourself, and choosing to align with love. And then, notice from a neutral perspective how others are responding and how they are showing up. Are they calibrating to this? If not, what is the act of love for yourself? This aligns with what is from love for others, what is for the highest and best for others as well.

When you are the one who recognizes what is not coming from love, it is also your opportunity to shift the pattern overall—to be the living example of love. This is a healing opportunity for all involved. It is not your responsibility to manage other people's triggers when their addiction to anger, sadness, and fighting is not further fueled. Because this is what it is to stay in these unhealthy dynamics—enabling the addiction to lower frequencies. And so, the healing comes when you choose differently, when you show up differently, when you source and act from love. When you do, there is new fuel. Are you calibrating to those around you, or are you offering them space to calibrate to you? If they are calibrating to you, at what frequency have you set the tone?

CHAPTER 18

SETTING BOUNDARIES

Many misunderstand setting boundaries to mean avoiding, rejecting, or acting from anger, fear, or resentment. This is not setting a boundary. A boundary is not avoidance. It is not a barrier. It is clarity in how you wish to feel, in how you will show up, in what you will engage in and what you will not, in what you require to consistently show up as the truest, most authentic, most loving version of yourself. This requires you to know yourself well, to know what you require, and to know what is most supportive for you and what is not, so that you can act from this knowing, uphold that frequency, and be able to communicate with your energy what you are available for and what you are not. Boundaries are gifts for you and all others, as they are pillars that support the effortless maintenance of higher frequencies.

Boundaries allow the energy to calibrate to a higher frequency within any dynamic. Think of it as a bolster propping you up in the higher realms.

When you are clear with your own boundaries, which are really energetic requirements for yourself, you direct the flow of energy in a way that feels fully aligned for you, and you will palpably notice the ease, grace, and love that appears in your life. Boundaries are clarity. They are portals that allow in that which is in alignment with love, and they are gatekeepers to redirect that which is not supportive for you elsewhere. But to set up a barrier instead of a boundary, to divert to avoidance instead of clarity with your boundaries for yourself and others, points to where else you might be avoiding things you do not want to look at, where you are afraid of speaking your truth, where you are afraid of showing your most authentic self, and where you would rather avoid your own needs than affect other people.

And so, what is your relationship with boundaries mirroring to you? Where are you more comfortable living for other people instead of for yourself? Where have you gotten used to calibrating to everyone else's vibration rather than upholding your own highest frequency? Rather than emitting your own most authentic energetic signature? Where are you hiding? What else are you avoiding saying, feeling, looking at, exploring? Where are you afraid of your own truths and your own needs? This is where you are still caught in illusion. This is where you are abdicating your power to direct energy flow in your own life. Many misunderstand boundaries because they are looking from the lens of an all-or-nothing mindset, when, in fact, the boundary allows you to more effortlessly live in between.

The issue is not really the boundary, but the lens. Where else is an all-or-nothing attitude limiting your perception of possibilities? Your relationship with boundaries will reflect to you exactly where you are still living in fear, illusion, and limitation. To be clear with your energetic boundaries is to claim the maintenance of a higher vibration, as you are taking responsibility for your energy field and overall frequency. Remember that your energy field is your responsibility. How will you take care of it? If you have been perceiving a boundary as what keeps others out, then perhaps it is not a boundary at all. Perhaps it is the fear of stepping into your power. Perhaps it is the fear of truth. Perhaps it is the projection of someone who benefits from energetic enmeshment and codependency.

To shift a dynamic through avoidance, rejection, or acting from anger, fear, or resentment is not love. It is that simple, but the application is more complex. It is first anchoring into love for yourself—*what is the way to move forward from full love for myself and for others?* Not obligation. Not expectation. Where is that from? Not comfortability. Not just what you are used to. Divine love! We understand that many block themselves from relating to biological family differently because they are viewing it from an all-or-nothing perspective, and this need not be so. Dynamics always shift and change. But just like in a romantic partnership, there are certain wounds it will be more productive to heal on your own first, and then you are able to re-enter a relationship from a healed place. And what was "unhealthy" before, what was not a vibrational match, what was not anchored in love, can completely shift. It doesn't always, but sometimes it does! That is the natural flow of energy in the universe—always flowing.

There is always opportunity for change. But it requires you to choose it, and not everyone does. You must honor what is true now—not what was true before, or what could be. There are infinite possibilities of what could be. What is real is now. This is living in the present. When you hold onto dynamics because of what was, you are staying stuck in the past. When you hold onto how the dynamic could be, you are living in a possible future. Neither is the truth of the now. What is the truth of the now is how you are feeling now and what you are available for now.

CHAPTER 19

ENERGETIC TOXINS

Relationships are the biggest blocks, and conversely, the biggest activators, for most of you when it comes to manifestation in general. You might not realize that your family, friendships, lovers, career, health, inspiration, creativity, mood, and spiritual gifts are all connected. It is all energy. You are always exchanging energy, shifting energy, and feeling energy. If you recognize the environmental and nutritional pollutants in your world, and then choose to shift your diet and lifestyle in order to support the health of your body, what about your energetic health? A toxic conversation is still a toxin.

To hold onto energetic cords rooted in shame, guilt, resentment, and judgment are toxins to your energy body, holding your frequency down. When you keep your frequency low, your health is impacted, your career is impacted, your creativity is impacted, your mood is impacted, flow is impacted, and your relationships are impacted. Your ability to align with love, money, health, and wealth in all of its forms are impacted. Your mental health often suffers. When you are consistently attached to vibrations that are not in alignment with your truth and with love, you are given signals from within that something must change.

Your body is trying to support you by guiding you to release what is not in alignment with your truth. This could be through extra weight you are carrying, skin irritation or blemishes, anxiety, depression, chronic illness, blood sugar imbalances, disease related to any organ, chronic symptoms of any sort...the list goes on. Exploring what is out of alignment in the system must include misaligned relationships. What is not in alignment with love that is being fed to your system will dull your frequency, and at a certain point can create sickness in the body. "Incurable" diseases and diseases of aging must be looked at anew.

You know when something is off! Understand that everyone you have a relationship with has an energetic cord with you. There is a dynamic when you are energetically connected with or attached to that person that can be like fuel to a car. What is the quality of the fuel? If you resent someone or someone resents you, the frequency is felt by both, and this affects your overall magnetism. This affects your physical energy, your mood, and all aspects of life, because it is affecting your vibration.

Take stock of all energetic cords and feel into the vibration of each from a neutral perspective. When the frequency is not in alignment with love, open yourself to the question, what is feeding the dynamic? Where are you not acting from unconditional love? How do you feel in relation to them? The only way to fully see the truth is to align with truth yourself and to show up with love yourself. The rest reveals itself. When you align with divine love and maintain that frequency, whatever is left is a clearer representation of the cord. From this awareness, you can set the intention to shift the energy. If another is feeding the cord with anger or resentment, for example, that is their choice, but you can make the choice to shift your own vibration, to maintain the higher frequency, to transmute that energy, and to not accept or keep that frequency in your field. From there, it need not affect you anymore. But this requires awareness, and the clear choice to uphold a different frequency. Make the energetic decision, and the physical decisions will follow.

CHAPTER 20

THE FREQUENCY OF RELATIONSHIPS

Imperfection is a part of the human experience, and a perfect aspect, from our perspective. And so, we are not suggesting you expect people to be "perfect" as you might understand the term. We perceive the term differently, as we view imperfection as part of the perfection of all that is. But when you see people from love, you perceive their actions differently. You see them from your heart instead of from your wounds. What we would like to offer you is a different way of perceiving relationships and the frequency of each. It is the energetic sum that creates the frequency, not the individual components. In fact, the relationships that are rooted most deeply and clearly in love will have the skillset and love to move through disagreements, conflict, or low-frequency emotions. It is not necessarily that those experiences will be absent.

The comparison we will offer is understanding your own vibrational frequency, which is not simply one thought, action, or emotion. For example, feeling sad or angry does not make you a low-frequency being—it is an energy passing through. If there is one rainy day in California, does that mean California has become a rainy state overall? No. And so, what we will ask you to tune into is the overall frequency of the dynamic. Challenges that present themselves in relationships can be an opportunity for the relationship itself to expand into its next level of depth and love, the same way that challenging experiences offer that to you as an individual.

And so, what is the theme? What is the consistent emotion? What is the foundational frequency of the relationship? When you are operating from divine love in relationships, you will automatically feel encouraged to approach conflict or hurt from a different perspective and energy. But how often is the conflict created because someone is looking to make the other person wrong or themselves right? Who is expecting someone to hurt or betray them, and so they are perceiving the situation from this place? You cannot control how another meets you, but you do choose which energy you meet them from and with. You can choose to align with harmony or discord. When you choose love, when you choose healing, when you choose forgiveness, there is space to see each other another way. To come from a place of compassion. To offer everyone a learning opportunity. This is where you come to understand what it would look like to create positive change in your life. You cannot force someone else to choose to act from love, but you can choose what vibration you hold. How is it you wish to inspire others? What is the energetic imprint you wish to leave?

On the other side of this is the awareness of how you show up in relationships. Again, you might invite in the perspective of, *what if I viewed all dynamics as simply reflections through which I can learn how I show up, and how I respond?* This allows you to move from a place of unconscious reaction to conscious response. If you are committed to aligning with love, you will start to become aware of why you choose the way you choose, why you behave the way you behave, and why you say the things you say. What behaviors are you engaging in because you are looking for someone else's attention? For someone else's approval? For someone else's love? This is pointing to where you have forgotten your wholeness, where you are still sourcing from outside yourself, where there is a piece of you that is still yearning for love, care, and nourishment, where you might be projecting something from your past onto another, or where you might be abdicating responsibility for your feelings or healing. There are many possibilities, but we point this out because many of the behaviors that seem to instigate conflict come from the place of desiring attention. This is helpful to notice, in fact, because it brings attention to a piece of yourself that would like some love, care, and attention.

Here we see other layers of codependency. What would it look like for you to relate from a place of not needing anyone, in the sense of not needing them to feel good or whole, but rather, simply enjoying being in their presence? What would it look like for you to relate from a place of not needing attention, because you give plenty of attention to all of yourself? What would it look like for you to relate from a place of not needing love from someone outside of yourself? Of not needing from a place of lack, but desiring from a place of expansion, excitement, and curiosity? What a relief on both sides!

From this you start to pay attention to—what do we bond over? What is the frequency of the conversation? There will be certain dynamics where you feel you cannot go deeper. You cannot go further. You feel a cap on where it can go. That limitation is showing you something about the relationship. Again, what is the frequency of the conversation? Where do you bond over complaining or gossip? Where do you bond only over pain or struggles? If this is the energy that feeds the relationship, you will unintentionally, or perhaps intentionally, attract more situations to complain about, or perhaps not even attract, but perceive situations from the energy of complaining, because what else do you talk about? If that is the frequency the relationship is built on, if that is the foundation, if that is the connection point, then to maintain the relationship you will experience more of the same. What are you discussing with your loved ones, the ones you keep close to you? How does the conversation make you feel? Pay attention to where you feel drained and low, and where you feel lit up, inspired, and expanded.

To be clear, to express frustration does not necessarily mean the entire relationship is built on bonding over complaining. You can express frustration from a place of sharing, opening your heart, and moving the energy. But when this is the general pattern, you will feel heavy consistently. This is an opportunity to shift the dynamic, to show up differently, to ingrain a new frequency, which is an opportunity for the other person as well. Most conversation dynamics are simply what people are used to, but those can be changed. If you are not satisfied with the dynamic of the conversation, shift it yourself. This is how you direct the energy. You must make a shift to create a shift. Where are you blaming others for your unhappiness? It is not up to them—it is up to you. Remember how powerful you are!

If you desire the frequency of the relationship to shift, show up differently. Hold a different frequency in the dynamic, in the conversation. It might take a beat for the other person to recalibrate, but if they are truly in alignment with you in your most expanded state, they will recalibrate in their own time. Many relationships transform quite beautifully in this process! This is growth in tandem. But how can you clearly evaluate a relationship if you have not set up the energetic container to align with the frequency you desire to begin with? You are not able to see the truth of what can be until you show up in the relationship in the way you wish to feel, fully as yourself—as your most authentic, loving self, at your highest, purest frequency. Allow the dynamic to recalibrate. From there, you can see what is aligned and what is not.

CHAPTER 21

LEANING IN

From here we would like to clarify a few points about "needing" people, as we have mentioned above. It is also easy to accidentally swing too far to the other side of the spectrum, to be so anchored in not "needing" anyone that you are rooted in an inauthentic energy of hyper-independence, which is often another way to keep people out because you are afraid of being hurt, being fully seen, or being perceived as weak. Your truth is love and authenticity, and a critical point of your human experience is to connect—to learn more about yourself and the world through points of connection, through different experiences, through relationships. This is core to who you are and how you collect experiences. But it is how you show up in relationships that is key. It is through relationships that you deepen your connection with Source, with oneness. There is much to be done individually, but it is through connection with others that you find yourself closer to complete oneness, that you find clear reflections of expansion and growth points within yourself. This is how you remember aspects of yourself that you have perhaps forgotten.

You might also use the term "needing someone" to mean desiring a connection with someone from a place of knowing your wholeness, from a place of sovereignty, and recognizing that there is a core "need" to connect in order to deepen your experience here and squeeze the most out of this experience. However, this is quite different from "needing" someone to fill in places that you feel are deficient, to abdicate responsibility for yourself and put it on another, to keep yourself busy, to avoid things that are for your highest and best to explore, to source love from another instead of recognizing it within yourself. The difference is connecting and relating from an empowered, whole, conscious place rather than a disempowered space. Do you feel empowered and whole within yourself first? Or are you looking for someone else to give you what you think you want and need? To need from the ego is different than to a desire from the soul. To need from the ego is quite different from the soul-led desire for connection, and the soul-led desire to enrich your experience here, to deepen your understanding of yourself, to deepen your connection to Source, to more fully embody your essence as love, and to more clearly embody your authenticity.

Within that connection, you share from a place of vulnerability, opening your heart, and sharing your heart—not looking for someone to fix you, because you are rooted in the knowing that you are whole, that you have the answers you need, and that you are fully supported. It is a beautiful thing to share and to ask for support, to lean in when you need it. But the key is to be aware of the energy from which you share. One might accidentally fall into codependency or wanting to be fixed just as easily as they might fall into hyper-independence, pushing everyone out because they are afraid to share the truth in their hearts.

What we will point out is this—the more you are in your wholeness, the more you are connected to your intuition, to your soul, to your innate wisdom, you might find that sharing and leaning in look a bit different. There will be far less you ask for advice about, as many of you relate through asking for advice from other people, because you are scared to listen to your own intuition, or you don't want to seem like you know it all. As the voice of your soul becomes louder and clearer, you will know what to do, you will be clear in the next steps, and so sharing or asking for support will feel different and might look different. You will spend less time asking for help when you share with others, and more time sharing your desires, your dreams, what you are excited about, what you are curious about, and what you are inspired about. The energy will be less about "fixing problems"—as many of you relate in this way—and more about sharing from the heart space. When you are going through a difficult time, expressing your feelings is a gift of sharing your heart, of allowing yourself to be seen in all frequencies, of allowing all of yourself to be held and loved. It is sharing your heart as a gift, not sharing it for attention or looking to be fixed.

Is it wrong to ask for advice from another? Of course not! You each hold unique perspectives and unique divine wisdom—you are here to share, to learn from each other, to expand each other, and to support each other! But what is the energy from which you ask? Are you asking for help, advice, or support from a place of illusion—believing you are not enough? Are you asking for advice from a place of giving your power away, or from a place of genuine curiosity because you would like to hear another perspective? This is an important skill to develop—to be able to receive information and opinions without giving your power away to them, but rather holding your confidence and simply taking it in as information and perspective. Then, you can tune into whether or not it aligns with your truth. Understand that asking for support or advice is a sign of respect, an opening of the heart. Asking for support or advice when aligned with divine love does not include giving away your power, abdicating your personal responsibility, or forgetting your own inner knowing. You will recognize that other perspectives are simply additional information to consider as you tune into what is for your highest and best.

In fact, this is an important part of connection. As you all have different experiences, different life paths, different perspectives, and your own conditioning, it is most helpful to explore those other experiences and perspectives to broaden your own realm of possibility, to see things another way, to notice where you have been only seeing from one angle when there are many others to consider. That does not mean taking on the lens of another, but simply recognizing more possibilities. This expands your consciousness. This is a different way of relating. It is rooted in your confidence, your own intuition, your own knowing, your own wholeness, and your own abilities. It acknowledges that you are safe to be fully seen at all stages, that you are endlessly deserving of love and support.

Sometimes, it is in a moment when you are caught in limiting beliefs or illusions that leaning into support and love is a crucial step in shining a light to remind you of your truth—your essence as love, that you are supported, that you are seen, that you are loved. You need not do it all yourself or figure it all out yourself. This is why you have connection points, expansion points, support all around you, as Source is within all and works through all. But to engage with support from wholeness, love, and opening your heart instead of looking to be fixed or abdicating responsibility is a key distinction. And so, sharing your heart and holding space for another are beautiful forms of energy exchange that deepen and expand the connection. It is that frequency of sharing that allows you to go deeper into your experience with another. As you are more fully seen, you feel the love of Source itself.

When you are vulnerable from a place of love, from a place of no expectations, from a place of simply sharing your heart as a point of connection, this is a beautiful gift! This is an expression of divine love. It offers the opportunity for you to see who is ready to embrace that frequency, who can see that gift as the expression of divine love it is, who receives it with love and care, who is a direct vibrational match for you when you clearly express your truest frequency. And so, the line between codependency and leaning in to open up a deeper connection is in the foundational frequency—the energy of the intention itself. How does it feel? Codependency pulls, tugs, pokes, and feels like a heavy weight, an energy drain. Leaning in, sharing, welcoming in support is a welcoming in of divine love, a recognition of your inherent worthiness to receive love, a loving gift that is an expression of the divine —it deepens, it softens, it enriches, it expands, it inspires.

CHAPTER 22

THE ENERGETICS
OF ATTRACTION

Next, we will explore the energetics of attraction, to allow this to move to conscious awareness. What we will also remind you of is that as you understand attraction more, there is a balance between more deeply understanding yourself and being aware, while also not moving into a place of overthinking and blocking your emotions, because your emotions are valuable information as well. There is not always a linear explanation for your emotions. It is all information that is helpful, and so we invite you to take it all into consideration. Why the emotions and feelings are important is because they guide you to your soul's desires and to the lessons you are meant to learn. But conscious thoughts and awareness are important so you can identify which emotions are actually the voice of your soul, and which emotions are expressions of the ego—of fear, of expectation, of self-fulfilling prophecies.

Why are you drawn to the things you are drawn to? You will be drawn to different people based on your frequency. You will be drawn to different people and perceive your emotions differently depending on if you are living and interpreting from your ego, your mind, your conditioning, or if you are living and interpreting from your soul. You will be drawn to different people based on how clearly you are living your truth and your authenticity, which requires knowing yourself and understanding what actions are coming from a place of wanting attention, of wanting someone else to be the source for you, of avoiding looking at things within yourself. The attraction will shift.

And so, the clearest path to attracting the most aligned relationships of all sorts that are resonant with the truest expression of your soul, the ones where you are seen so clearly and loved so truly, is to focus on living your truth, following your soul, perceiving from love, and being your most authentic self. Yes, it is that simple. But if you are still caught up in illusions, you will attract illusions. If you are still living illusions, you will feel illusions. Align with your truth, align with love, and the truth of relationships will be revealed. It will be clear to you what is a match and what is not. And so you will find that the time it takes to know if someone is a match or not shortens, because the clearer you are with yourself, the clearer it is as to who is a fit and who is not. It does not necessarily take the "time" you think it needs to. Living your truth—being your most authentic self—is the light that sheds the truth of dynamics. The time truly required for an accurate perception of a relationship will depend on your vibration, level of self-awareness, connection to your intuition, and soul alignment.

Here is the catch—many think they know themselves when they do not. They know themselves on a surface level. They know an old version of themselves. They know the version of themselves other people know. They know themselves from the place of the mind and the ego, rather than knowing themselves on the soul level, knowing themselves from the lens of the highest truth. And so what many identify as instant soul resonance is more like ego resonance. It is more like instant gratification—getting the hit of an addiction they have yet to break, or a filling in of what they are not sourcing themselves. A drug that activates them for a moment, but then the energy dulls.

And so, you must be honest with where you truly know yourself and where you might not. The insights available from previous relationships are your key! When you reflect back on relationships of all types—friendships, romantic partners, family dynamics, business relationships—allow yourself to explore why you were attracted to that relationship to begin with. How did it make you feel? How was it serving you? You might realize that you were attracted to familiarity, but what is familiar is not necessarily aligned with your highest frequency. What is familiar is also often what you will outgrow, if you are committed to the path of expansion. What is familiar can be what was familiar to the younger version of you. It might be familiar because it was a similar frequency to that of your previous partner, to that of your father, to that of your mother, to that of an old friend.

When you've already done it before, when you've already experienced it before, it initially feels more comfortable—but big picture, will it lead to the repetition of a dynamic that was not necessarily for your highest and best? Who or what does it remind you of? How does the dynamic make you feel? Do you know how to source this from Source itself? Is there an energy of dependency? Or curiosity? What need is it filling that makes you feel safe, or boosts your ego? Do you like to be needed? Do you like the boost in confidence? Is it filling a void? Is it filling your loneliness? Notice the gap between what it is filling and what you actually desire in a relationship.

As you shift, as you change, as you grow, what you desire might as well. And when we say desire, we mean on a soul level, which can be different from your ego desire. Often what you "need" in terms of aligning with a soul desire is not necessarily what your ego wants, because the relationship expands you! It is not always familiar or comfortable. Have you subconsciously decided that familiar and comfortable are ideal? If you haven't already experienced what you desire, then when you meet it, it will be uncomfortable and unfamiliar in some way.

We invite you to take the negative connotations out of these words, and instead get curious. What is this bringing out within me? What is different here that I haven't experienced before? What opportunities are available here for me to explore another part of myself? It is from this curiosity that you will get clearer answers from your inner knowing. It is also from this place of curiosity that you will realize if the vibration is truly not a match in the sense of not being supportive for what feels true for you in this moment versus not a match in the sense of not aligned with the current version of you but fully aligned with the more expanded, authentic version of you.

What is not familiar—what is different—will not always feel comfortable, because it is new. But it must feel "new" if you want to enter a new dynamic. If you have not yet experienced that which you truly desire in a relationship before, then expect it to feel different! Your clearest comparison point will be the frequency of divine love from Source itself. When you are perceiving from the place of the ego, conditioning, the mind, and your wounds, you will be attracted to familiarity. When you are perceiving from the place of the soul, from love, from truth, from your most authentic frequency, you will be attracted to that which is aligned with divine love, truth, and authentic soul resonance.

Here is yet another nuance. Many of you have had an experience of not feeling resonant with a person at first who, over time, became someone you did feel resonant with. And so, when you feel the vibrational gap, in which direction does that go? Is the nonresonance based on the mind or the soul? Is the nonresonance based on who you were, who you are now, or the more expanded version of you? Is the nonresonance actually a judgment of someone else who is highlighting something that you desire, crave more of, or don't like about yourself? Is the nonresonance actually a judgment of someone else who is reflecting a frequency you are not yet comfortable with because you are not comfortable with it within yourself? Confidence, truth, divine love? Many actually push away those who embody these energies because they are not familiar with these frequencies yet within themselves or within their relationships. These energies can feel threatening, uncomfortable, or even unsafe to someone who has never encountered them before in relationships. Notice your tendency to fear the unknown and unfamiliar.

This is similar to how many people push away dynamics based in real, divine, unconditional love because all they have known are codependent or dramatic relationships. What would it look like for there not to be drama? For there not to be a problem to always solve, or something to always fix? You say you desire this, but where do you push away the opportunities for it? This is where you see the addiction to the drama and to keeping yourself busy. And again, do you feel safe to receive? To simply receive love without attachment? To be in peace? To allow peace to be your state, rather than requiring and thus creating situations that feel tumultuous and need not be so? These are important questions to consider.

The relationships that truly expand you will feel different. They will pull out something new from within you. This is not from the other person—it is from within you. If you are aligned with your expansion and growth, of course you will attract in people of a higher frequency that give you an opportunity to recalibrate to a higher vibration yourself. When these people come in, you will not yet be used to their frequency! However, the more time you spend getting familiar with Source, connecting to Source, sitting in divine love, the expansive frequencies will feel more comfortable and familiar. This is when you will be able to clearly recognize what is a soul-aligned match instantly instead of feeling triggered or unsettled when you meet that frequency. The difference in perception depends on how familiar you are with the frequency of divine love, with the frequency of truth, with your most authentic soul frequency.

CHAPTER 23

CLEAR COMMUNICATION

Notice as you relate—are you drawn to the actual dynamic of the relationship, the actual frequency of the person and that of the relationship itself, or the illusions you are projecting onto it? For much of the attraction people feel is because of the projections. You are a powerful creator, but this can also manifest as stories about others, stories that you project onto that person—that they are in love with you, that they're not, that they are going to hurt you, that they never would, that they're acting a certain way for a certain reason, that they have certain judgments or expectations…the stories go on and on! Most of your relationship dynamics are in fact driven by stories and illusions rather than clear communication that allows space for the truth of what is to come to light. This is why many of you become confused. You will notice a remarkable difference in your perception when you stop perceiving from stories, expectations, illusions, judgments, past experiences, and future ideals, and start perceiving from the truth of the now.

Get clear with what is a story and what is not. What are your own beliefs and expectations? What is your mind telling you? What is your heart telling you? What is your soul telling you? What are your true emotions? What are your true emotions when you release projections from the past? When you release expectations about how someone or something will be delivered? When you get out of your head and into your heart? And then, what has been revealed to you in how that person shows up? This is about recognizing your own energetic awareness about the other person—the energy that you feel—if you are clear in this discernment for yourself. This is also about recognizing what they have said and how they have acted. And if you have a question or are wondering something about the relationship or the other person, are you creating stories in your mind, or are you communicating clearly?

Much of the confusion and the proliferation of illusory stories are simply because you are not expressing clearly. You are not asking. You are not sharing. What if instead of creating illusions in your head, you were direct and clear? Here is where you are afraid to express yourself, because you anticipate judgment or rejection or being perceived as "too much." There is your opportunity to speak more kindly to yourself, to see where you can further align with unconditional love, where you can remember your inherent worth and deservingness, where you can align with your confidence as an extension of Source and remember that clear communication is love.

There is no such thing as "too much" when you are comfortable with abundance, when you are comfortable with Source, all that is, and when you remember the beauty, power, and love in your fullest, clearest expression. We invite you to get curious about the energy underneath perceiving something or someone as being "too much." What is the line of "just enough" according to that perception? Within the phrase itself is an energy of limitation. Be all of yourself. Receive love fully. We invite you to embrace the energy of "more," rather than arbitrary limitations that are just extensions of fear of your own power.

But where there is much dissonance in relationships is because of unclear communication, creating stories and expecting things to go a certain way, or adjusting yourself to make others "like" you. When you do that, are you surprised at how it ends up? Not feeling the way you thought? Still craving more? Are you left feeling trapped or unsatisfied? If adjusting yourself is what allows someone to "like" you, then they don't really at all—they like your illusions. They don't see the real you. This is where you feel loneliness. The only way to attract an authentic match is to be your authentic self.

The answer is simple—truth. Honesty. Love. Allow others to express their truth, and you won't have a need to create stories. If you're looking for an answer, why not go directly to the source? You can waste your time trying to find a historical date in a math book, or you can open up the history book. Where you waste your time in the math book is where you are afraid of truth. Why do you feel safer not knowing? Why do you feel safer in your stories? This is a false sense of safety—a comfort for the ego, but a denial of the greatest gifts available to you!

What if you allowed your reality to be as beautiful, magical, and expansive as possible? You can allow that to be your reality through truth, through love, and by living in the present. Or, you can stay in the stories of your mind, while you feel the dissonance in your reality. You can continue to project your past onto your now, aligning yourself with a future that is just another iteration of the past. Let yourself live your dreams. Let yourself live the love that you so desperately wish to experience! This can only be done by being this yourself. Living as love— being love—is opening the space for truth, living truth, and expressing truth.

And so, where you are attached to the stories might also be where you are attached to the games, the chase—entertaining yourself in this way, keeping yourself busy in this way. Craving the ego hit, the instant gratification, the comfort of staying the same because you fear true depth, true connection, being fully seen. How does that feel? Are the games from love? You wonder why you attract the type of relationships that you do, yet you still engage in the games, the back and forth, pretending. Pretending to not feel the way you really do. What do you think will be the result when coming from that place?

If you wish to create an experience of a certain vibration, the foundational frequency must be of that vibration. To operate truly from love for others, ask yourself—*is it loving to pretend? Who is this serving, and in what way?* For you will see how in trying to people-please, or adjusting yourself to get what you want, you are not acting from divine love for all others. And then, what do you expect to attract? This might show up in your relationships or in another area of your life, but understand the energy of your choices. It is the intention, the honest intention, that determines the frequency. The truth of the vibration of every relationship will always be revealed. You can choose to see it now or later. The longer you wait to acknowledge it, the more time the frequency has time to amplify, to build, to gain momentum.

CHAPTER 24

A NEW RELATIONSHIP TEMPLATE

As more of you relate to each other from unconditional love, a new type of relationship will be created. There will be new norms. But it will start with a shift in recognizing what you are drawn to and why, and in honoring your feelings. You might feel incredibly drawn to someone you wouldn't expect to be—perhaps the package is delivered in a way you didn't anticipate! You might recognize that someone who triggered you before is one of your greatest teachers—for whenever we are reminded of a deep truth within, it will leave an energetic impact. It depends on the situation as to whether it serves us or not to continue that relationship.

We point this out because the biggest block for most in relationships right now is they are expecting to "know" when they meet the aligned frequency, but they aren't tuned into soul-level knowing. Rather, they are determining "knowing" based on what they felt before (we wonder how that worked out), and what stories or expectations they have created consciously or unconsciously in their minds. Be open to the unexpected. Do not limit yourself with your expectations—this is where you choose settling. Everything you desire might come in exactly when you least expect it, in the way you least expect it, at the time you least expect it, because you are unattached. Because you are so aligned within yourself. Because you are living the vibration that is a match for divine love to drop directly in your field as a byproduct.

What you seek is there, energetically waiting for an opening. And so, you might desperately be looking on the first floor when the aligned match is on the ninth. And when you get to the ninth, are you truly seeing with an open heart, mind, and eyes, or are you running right past it, because you expect it to be a certain way? You need not know what the delivery looks like. In fact, this is where you limit yourself. Allow yourself to be surprised, and trust that your soul is guiding you to the perfect vibrational match. For this is the way that energy flows. Allow yourself to be open to what is different, as what you desire next is different from what you had or have, is it not? Allow yourself to be expanded—this stretches you into your fullest expression, your truest self.

What if, instead of looking, you focused on attracting? Remember how magnetic you are. You are always magnetizing that which is a vibrational match for you, and you can use this to your advantage! Many spend a lot of time looking, which is coming from their mind, ego, and conditioning. They believe they have to "go out and get it," when really what they must do is focus on being the clearest, truest versions of themselves. What if instead of depending on a dating app algorithm, you use your vibration as your algorithm? It never fails. The more you focus on living your truth, your joy, emitting your purest, most authentic frequency, following your inspiration, trusting your intuition, feeling lit up in your life, being the most you you can be, and aligning with your soul-aligned truth, what is for you comes straight to you. It will be delivered. And through that process you will have a clear knowing, because you will be so in tune with the voice of your soul—your intuition—and you will be so used to the frequency of divine love that is within you, because you have focused on being it, that you will recognize when the aligned match drops in your field. You will not miss it because you will know that the most effective relationship algorithm is embodying your truest, purest, unique frequency and living from that space, and then following your intuition, no matter where it leads you, even if your mind does not understand how it is connected.

Open yourself up energetically and emotionally. Live from the energy of love. Love yourself. Date yourself. Live the life you will live when with your partner. Get comfortable being all of yourself—this is how you open the space for the universe to deliver that which is exactly for you! When you are in the energy of looking, or of wanting, it is easy for you to shift into looking from the mind, from the ego, and from conditioning. It is easy for you to get in the energy of wanting, which creates a vibrational gap between you and that thing. It is easy for you to unintentionally shift into the energy of lack—of focusing on what you don't have—and then you attract more of the same. Maintain the frequency of divine love, of abundance, of joy, of excitement. Maintain your truest, most authentic frequency. Be all of you, and then follow your intuition. Create space in your life for that which you desire to come in—space in your home, space in your schedule, emotional space to meet someone deeply, to see them deeply, to hold space, to fully share yourself with them. Get ready, because they are on their way! You must simply align with them.

Many of you might find that you unintentionally shift into a disempowered, disappointed space when you use other methods to find the aligned person, because you are in an energy of forcing, of looking, of seeking, or of needing something you don't have, of lack, rather than receiving, staying open, and maintaining the frequency you wish to attract more of. When you understand the energetics of vibrational attraction from a manifestation perspective, you know how to simply align with that which you are calling in. And so, perhaps utilizing a dating service is a pathway your soul self will take you on as a way of aligning you with a vibrational match for the purest version of you. The key is to ask yourself why you are doing what you are doing. Was it because it was intuitively inspired from a soul-aligned space? Was it synchronistic and an intuitive yes? Or was it because you're afraid you will be alone? Because you are afraid you won't find someone? Because you are thinking and being from a place of lack and scarcity, and taking action from that place of fear, from the mind, from the ego? Let your soul guide you! When you are in the latter energy, do not be surprised when what you attract in is also vibrating with scarcity energy.

Relationships seem to be the place where many of you accidentally fall back into fears, illusions, forgetting your power, and thinking you are alone. Hold your true vibration. Trust yourself. Remember how magnetic you are. This is your test of energetic resilience. It is one thing to hold your frequency alone in your room with no one around—it is another to be energetically resilient enough to hold that frequency when in the energy field of others. It is in relationships where you see the truth of how energetically resilient you are, as you start to adjust to another's frequency, as you own certain feelings and emotions that are truly that of another. It is in dating and new relationships that many of you feel you have lost your minds! You have not lost your minds—but you are feeling the power of emotions. You are picking up intuitive signals, whether or not you label them as such. You are feeling how potent love is, desire is, love is. You are feeling the intensity of frequency. And you often confuse energies from those around you with your own, as energy is more easily picked up on and transferred when you open your energy field in the context of building a new relationship.

And so, notice what is yours and what is not. Notice where you are adjusting your vibration to calibrate to another rather than upholding your own frequency. Adjusting your vibration to calibrate to another might manifest as adjusting your expectations, your needs, your style of communication, and so on to align with the person you are with. Is that really you? Stay true to yourself. Uphold your frequency. This is how you attract in the most aligned, authentic match.

And we will also add that part of attracting the most aligned match is staying rooted in the knowing that what you are desiring is being delivered, including each part of that process. What we mean by this is part of the process of attracting your most aligned match is learning all of the lessons required for you to fully be ready to receive that which is for your highest and best, which can come through in other relationships. We share this because once you set your intention, many of you expect the next person you connect with romantically to be your lifelong partner, and if they are not, you feel it is not working, you get discouraged, and you want to give up. This is missing the point. What is being delivered to you when you are anchored into divine love and your most authentic frequency is exactly what is required for you to be energetically ready and available for your most aligned match. It is all part of the process. And so, if it is required for you to untangle a certain energetic knot, to learn a certain lesson, to shift your energy in a way to be the exact match for someone who is for your highest and best, the lesson might be delivered through a different relationship.

We invite you to shift your perspective on dating, and this also extends to friendships. Every relationship is valuable. Every relationship is preparing you. Every relationship is teaching you, no matter how long the contract lasts. Just because it was not the "final result" as you might have planned does not mean it was not of the utmost importance, does not mean it was not necessary for the frequency to shift in order for you to align with your next relationship, does not mean that it was not worth your time. Where are you looking to skip ahead? Wanting to skip ahead is how you block yourself. You want to skip to high school before completing elementary school, but if you skipped to high school, you would be completely unprepared for your classes. You would be overwhelmed and confused, and the result would not be ideal. But if you went through the proper preparation, you would get excellent marks in your classes, experience the time with ease, and feel completely prepared for the next phase. Do you see how the "preparation" is also part of the journey? What is occurring now, what is coming through now, is exactly what is meant for you to focus on in the present.

Many of you live in the possibility of a future timeline, and in doing so, you miss your present. You miss the richness, the opportunities, the learning, the beauty. Find the beauty in every moment. When you are aligned with your highest, most authentic frequency, when you are living as love, all you must do is follow your intuition, follow each step one by one, and know that each step you are guided to is exactly where you are meant to be. We will remind you not to judge the journey. Your mind thinks it knows what the "next steps" are, but your soul knows what your mind cannot. When you have set your intention, and you energetically calibrate to your highest frequency, and you live as love, your reality will recalibrate. Everything is supporting you in that frequency, in that soul-aligned intention. Part of that recalibration includes the experiences required for you to be completely energetically available for that which you wish to attract. It would already be in your reality if you were truly a vibrational match, and so you will attract in the experiences that, if you choose to accept the opportunities, will support you in making the energetic shifts that will calibrate you to that frequency.

ATTACHMENT AND EXPECTATIONS

Trust your intuition. Trust your journey. Uphold your most authentic frequency, and it will all flow from there. You can always look at where you are now and wish you were there again, so enjoy it! You, in this moment, in this place, as you are now, are experiencing a unique vibrational mixture. In one week, one year, five years, you might look back and wonder why you did not relish in that mixture for longer. Enjoy your now. Recognize the purpose of connecting with different people, as all reflect something different for you. All teach you something different. If you are viewing dating or meeting new people from the lens of trying to reach an end result, you are missing the point. Is there an end result? Relationships often shift and change. Allow yourself to be fully in the experience of connecting with different energies, different frequencies, being fully present and aware, receiving the beauty of the moment and the exchange, fully learning whatever is available to you in the interaction, and simply enjoying connecting with different souls. Do you view a short relationship as a failure or a waste of time? It is nothing of the sort! It is a crucial step, a pivotal part of the journey, whether or not you see it in the current moment. How beautiful to get to connect with so many different souls and frequencies!

It is through fully receiving these connections, no matter how brief or long, that you are fully prepared for connections that are truly rooted in divine love. In fact, we find that many of you are not truly ready to receive the frequency of divine love because you are avoiding or ignoring the lessons available in the relationships gifted to you through your life that are meant to prepare you to receive this. If you are to play in the championship game, do you not treat every practice as that game? The player who treats the practice as just a practice, who does not fully embrace the opportunity to live in the energy of the championship game, is not fully prepared. It is the player who uses every practice as an opportunity to show up in the vibration of the championship game who enters that championship game prepared, ready, calm, excited, and ready to take on the challenge. If you avoid the lessons, opportunities, and practice now, you will not be prepared. We use the term "prepared" to refer to being a vibrational match. It is not a test in terms of worthiness, it is simply a matter of what is a frequency match and what is not.

There are countless opportunities in connecting with different souls—in experiencing different types of conversations, in having difficult conversations, in learning to speak up, in learning what you desire and what you do not in a relationship, in learning your own boundaries, in facing a variety of situations—to break apart any energetic knots that are holding your vibration down, to speak up and show up in an empowered way to raise your frequency, to expand further into your most authentic self. Each connection is an opportunity for a frequency upgrade, which aligns you with the highest frequency relationships available to you, but you must choose to take the opportunities. If you avoid them, then do not be surprised when you continue to attract in different versions of the same dynamic, or when you consistently feel the people you are attracting are not meeting you where you desire them to, or when you consistently feel a slight disconnect, or when you feel that it is not quite right, or when you feel like you're not attracting anyone at all (which is not true, but we understand you perceive it to be so). What lessons are you meant to learn? Which opportunities are you not taking? Where are you wanting to skip ahead? Look at what unfinished business you have from previous relationships, whether that be energetic or physical. Look at what you are attracting in your current reality and what opportunities are present for you. Is there a place where you can finally speak your truth, from your heart? Ask for what you need? Show up as the person you know you truly are? Hold space? Uphold a higher frequency? Be your most authentic self? Take the opportunity! It is only then that your frequency shifts, and you become energetically available for what is in your highest alignment.

It is from this space that you might learn to relate without attachment. It is the energetic attachment to an outcome that is another one of the biggest blocks for you in attracting aligned relationships. Your ego latches onto the idea that a specific person is your most aligned match when it might not be so, or that a situation is meant to transform a certain way or on a certain timeline when it might not be so. Notice where your ego is steering the ship! This is where you are still living in stories, and letting those stories and illusions guide you. This is why many of you feel you accidentally "lose" yourselves—because you are caught up in stories. Notice where your ego is attached. Where does this come from? Fear? Fear of not being enough? Fear of not finding someone else? Fear of being alone? Fear of not being chosen? Desperation? Lack? Scarcity? Settling? The deeper you go, you will finally face where the attachment comes from—and this is a piece of gold for you! This is exactly where you must look!

We will remind you that all is valuable, as it is all simply information. It is not that attachment is "bad," but rather that it is an energetic block to you receiving that which is for your highest and best because it anchors you into a specific frequency that is not the frequency of that which you are desiring. Therefore, it keeps you stuck. When you recognize you are in attachment, you can explore why on a deeper level, and this shows you exactly where you must look and what energetic knot you must untangle to align with your highest timeline and raise your frequency. This shows you what you get to release to embody your most authentic self. You might attach to a specific person or outcome, but what if that person or situation would not support you in feeling the way you wanted to feel all along?

Notice where you are attaching based on assumptions. The key is trusting your higher self, trusting your soul's guidance, and trusting vibrational alignment, which always aligns you with truth. This is why we invite you to meet consciously, for you never know who is going to shift your life in the most important ways. You never know who is going to help you unlock the most beautiful, expansive energies within. You never know who is exactly the person you have been waiting for, just delivered in a way or in a package you never expected. Release your expectations, and allow yourself to receive miracles. Allow yourself to be pleasantly surprised.

To go deeper into attachment is to explore expectations. What does it mean to relate without expectations? This is the new way of relating that many of you are stepping into as you shift your vibration and align with the divine definition of love. Many of you have expectations of other people and expectations in relationships that you are not consciously aware of, and so the key is to start to explore what expectations you might have that are hiding beneath the surface. Many of these expectations are based on conditioning of what was modeled to you or what someone else told you to expect. It is important to bring these to the surface so you can properly evaluate whether or not those expectations are in fact aligned with divine love and are in fact aligned with the relationships you truly desire to have. Many of these expectations are unconscious for you, and even the conscious ones are left unspoken. Bringing these expectations to the surface will offer an opportunity for you to explore exactly what you have been expecting of others, why you have been expecting it, and unconscious reasons why you have engaged in certain behaviors or latched onto certain beliefs about love.

It is within these expectations you can start to see what you have defined "love" as and what you have decided a loving relationship looks like. Has it been based on expectation? What we will offer to you, in alignment with the divine definition of love, is that divine love is without expectations. It is to love without condition. The conditions are the expectations. And so, are you willing to give and receive love without expectation? This is available to you when you remember where love comes from, when you realign with the unlimited source of love, when you choose to live and act as the love that you are. It is always available.

To love without expectation is distinct from knowing your boundaries, requirements, and needs in relationships. These boundaries, requirements, and needs are meant to be explored and set from your soul-self, not your ego, and they are an extension of what it looks like to uphold the frequency of divine love in your relationship container. To know this for yourself is key in maintaining your most authentic frequency and in building the muscle of energetic resilience. For the purposes of this exploration, we are differentiating standards from expectations. And so, understanding the requirements you have for what you are available for, based on the frequency of love, we see as different from loving with expectations in the sense of expecting someone to show up or respond in a certain way. The former is about you, the latter is about the other. When you are clear about your desires in a loving relationship, then you can simply offer space for others to calibrate to that dynamic and decide whether or not it is also aligned for them. Those who are truly soul resonant will either easily recalibrate or will already be calibrated. Allowing this opportunity is different from expecting someone to meet you where you are at or where you want to go. Where are your expectations secretly an attempt at controlling another's behavior? Expecting someone to calibrate to you is different than opening up the space for them to if they desire to, simply seeing if they do, from a neutral perspective. How does it feel for you when another expects you to calibrate to them?

This is about knowing your authentic code, living from that divine love, seeing what meets you there, and releasing what does not. Expectations from a place of setting intention for your own life are different from expectations for someone else from a place of trying to force them to show up in a certain way. The latter is where you are still in attachment, where you are attempting to control another, where you are in subtle resistance to their own free will choice, where it is mirroring to you what you are not meeting within yourself. When you meet your own requirements, when you show up for yourself, when you are anchored into your wholeness and your essence as divine love, is there a need to expect another person to show up a certain way for you?

Again, to hope, appreciate, and desire others to meet you there, to hold space for them to if they choose to, from a place of non-attachment, is different from needing them to and expecting them to from that place of need. This is an important point of differentiation, because expectations can come from an energy of divine love. The nuance comes from the foundational frequency. It can be in alignment with divine love to have "expectations" for yourself in terms of clear intentions for your life, as a way of grounding in the manifestation through maintaining the frequency. It can also be in alignment with divine love to have "expectations" for others to show up at that certain caliber of divine love as a way of holding the space for them to show up in their truth, because you truly see them on a soul level. But you will know the truth of the foundational frequency of the expectation based on if you feel as though you "need" another to meet that expectation in order for you to maintain your highest frequency, in order for you to feel loved and joyful. Notice where the expectation for another is from true divine love, is from seeing and knowing Source in that other being, as a way of holding the space for them to rise, as opposed to a requirement, a judgment, or an expectation because of your ego's needs.

Through this exploration, you see how attachment and expectations are connected, and how they are showing you exactly where you must look within yourself. Why are you so attached? What are you expecting from another, and why? Are you providing this for yourself? When you meet your own needs, when you tune inward and show up fully for yourself, when you are focused on your highest alignment and your sovereignty, you need not have expectations that someone else will do that for you. Rather, you are whole in yourself and clear in your own boundaries and requirements for what is aligned with your energetic field. You are energetically resilient and dedicated to upholding the frequency of love and your authentic energetic signature. You simply allow, and notice who aligns with this. Notice where your attachment and expectations are still feeding illusions and stories and are pointing to where you are living in the illusion of lack within yourself, where you are not meeting your own needs, where you are pointing the finger at another instead of turning inwards and exploring yourself. Notice where your attachment and expectations are a byproduct of trying to force something to work rather than allowing what is meant for you to flow to you. This is where you are letting ego get in the way, where you are not letting your soul self guide you to what is better than what you could have planned for, where you are unintentionally limiting yourself and your possibilities.

To release the attachment and the expectations is to release the limitations you put on yourself. And so, tune into what it would look like to truly give love, receive love, embody love, and live as love without expectation. To do so simply because it feels good for you, because it feels divine, because it is who you are when you embody your divinity, your essence as divine love, your essence as an extension of Source itself. It feels good. If it is not feeling good to give love without expectation, then we invite you to reflect on if it is truly divine love that you are sharing. Or is it something else? Is it divine love if it has conditions or expectations? If you believe that you must do something to earn love, you will expect this from others. And you will start to play the game—that one must show up in a certain way to deserve love, to earn love. With this line of thinking, you are in scarcity, you are in lack, you are in separation consciousness, you are disconnected from your essence as Source.

You are inherently deserving and worthy of love, because you are love. You are an extension of love. You get to choose to act as this and from this. And when you are fully anchored into this knowing of your inherent deservingness and worthiness as divine love, you see this in others. And there are no limits—there are no obligations to fulfill—to receive or give love.

THE LENS OF DIVINE LOVE

Remember, when you embody love and radiate it out, it is that frequency that fills you, and how incredible does that feel! It is truly living as an extension of Source—feeling that connection, experiencing the oneness that is love. When you live as love, when you embody divine love as a way of being, you feel Source moving through you, flowing through you, and working through you all the time. This is what you seek, on a core level—the remembrance, the oneness, the purest essence of love, to live as your most authentic self. This is what you crave to find through connection, but you must first embody it within yourself. If another withholds "love" because you have not met their own requirements, was that really love, in its divine form? Or was that obligation? And if you experience that dynamic, how do you meet it? Do you calibrate to that frequency, or do you uphold the frequency of love? Do you stay energetically resilient and strong? Do you transmute it? The relationships will only shift to their highest form if you show up differently, if you uphold your frequency, if you embody a different way of relating.

The more that you connect to your essence as love, the more you live from your soul self, the more you align with divine love and live authentically, you will notice that your perspective shifts all around. You will meet situations differently. You will see others differently. You will not be looking for the answer as to what is right and what is wrong. You will not be looking for the formula to achieve something. You will not be looking to categorize things into what is better or worse. You will move beyond this way of limited thinking. When you are anchored into divine love, when you see from this lens, when you fully embody this frequency, the perspective and action aligned with that vibration naturally flow through. You need not find the answer externally, and you need not wonder—you will follow your intuition, your inner knowing.

But for your inner knowing to naturally guide you to the perspective and action rooted in love requires the initial calibration to the frequency of divine love itself. From there, the answers flow. The knowing flows. You will notice that you show up differently. You respond differently. You see the love in others instead of looking to make them wrong or less than. You show up with compassion and understanding. You recognize it is not that they are "bad"— it is that in that moment, they were acting from or seeing from illusions, they forgot their essence as divine love, they were simply not living from their most authentic code. They were disconnected from the love in their own heart. You need not lower yourself into lower vibrations to react or respond, because you will recognize how nonresonant that feels.

When you know how good it feels to live as love, when you know how liberating and exhilarating it is to live truly as your most authentic self, why shift into any other vibration? It is effortless to uphold your truest frequency. It is exhausting to live from what is not. You are naturally a high-frequency being of love, which is why any time you are anchored into the lower frequencies, you will feel exhausted. You will feel dis-ease in the system. It is not aligned with your truth. And when you are in relationships that are not aligned with your authenticity, where you are not showing up as your most authentic self, where the energetic cord is not that of love and authenticity, you will feel tired. It will drain you. Anger, resentment, judgment, guilt, shame —these are exhausting. Because they are not your truth. They are an indicator that something is misaligned with your truest essence. When you are exhausted, this is showing where you are not calibrated to divine love, to authenticity. And so, notice where in your relationships you are feeling exhausted. Notice where you are feeling anger or sadness or guilt and shame. Here is where a shift is to be made. This starts with you.

As you relate without expectation and obligation, as you relate and see from the frequency of divine love, you will find that your relationships support your energy. You will find that you feel inspiration, joy, and excitement. When challenges arise and when there are lower vibrations to move through, you have the energy to do so, you have the knowing that you can and will, and you have the motivation to do so, because the frequency of love in the relationship is an infinite power source that moves you, that transforms, that heals, that energizes, that carries you through. And so we invite you to explore—where are you exhausted? Where are you drained? Where are you holding onto lower frequencies? This is where you limit yourself. Where do you only give "love" with conditions? Where do you have expectations of other people? What expectations do you have for yourself, and where do these come from? Why are you afraid to give love freely? Why are you afraid to receive love without conditions? Where are you not living as love yourself?

As you embody love and live as love, you will perceive differently. Your perspective will shift to be from the lens of divine love, and it is from this place that you will notice your attractions shift. When you are rooted in lower vibrations, how do you think you perceive? When you are perceiving from an energy of lack, of judgment, of guilt, of shame, of low self-worth, this will affect what you are attracted to, and what is attracted to you. This will affect what you are drawn to, because it will be a reflection of your frequency and the vibration of the lens through which you are perceiving. To first align with love, to first remember your self-worth, to first anchor into how incredible you are, to anchor into abundance and the beauty of all—this will shift what you notice in your reality, what you are drawn to, what is drawn to you, and how you perceive situations. What you might have thought was soul-level attraction before, you might then realize was actually resonance with your mask. What you might have thought was soul-level attraction before, you might then realize was addiction, was familiarity, was an unhealthy pattern, was lust, and so on. What you might have thought before was triggering, was frustrating, was undesirable, you might then view as expansive, as interesting, as inspiring, as attractive. The perspective shifts as the frequency shifts. The interpretation of events, conversations, and dynamics will shift as the frequency shifts. You can experience the same set of circumstances completely differently depending on your frequency.

The attraction will shift as your frequency shifts. Set your frequency first, anchor into the lens of divine love, see the love in others, anchor into the frequency of truth in your own life, and from here you will naturally perceive from that lens as well. But where you fear seeing the truth in yourself is where you will also not see the truth in others. Where you stay in illusion in your own life, where you lie to yourself in big and small places, this is where you have chosen the lens of illusion, and so you must not be surprised when you perceive relationship dynamics from the lens of illusion as well. To see the truth of what is a match and what is not, you must live from truth. To attract an honest relationship, you must anchor into honesty yourself first. To attract a relationship where both are seen and loved deeply, you must first see and love yourself deeply. Your relationship dynamics with others will simply reflect your relationship with yourself.

The power is in your hands. It is quite simple. Focus on embodying your divine essence as love, focus on emitting your most authentic frequency, and trust your soul's guidance. Remember, what you desire on a soul level is also desiring you. That which is a vibrational match for you is of course meant for you. It is up to you to calibrate to the frequency you desire so that you can easily magnetize each other. These are the matches that are truly soul-aligned, rather than ego-aligned. There is a distinct difference in depth of connection and opportunities for expansion in each. The relationships that are of vibrational resonance on a soul level when you are aligned with your most authentic energetic signature are those that connect you more clearly with the frequency of Source itself, with oneness, with pure love. This is what you seek, on a core level. It is why you desire connection, relationship—it is another manifestation of connection with Source. The relationships that are resonant with the ego, the mind, fear, and conditioning will deepen your connection with more of the same. This is where many of you feel blocked in your personal expansion, and you feel a deep craving for more. Does the connection allow the space for you to connect with oneness? With divine love? With Source itself? With your deepest truths? Some relationships are cloudy mirrors, and some are crystal clear. Some connections allow you to float, some allow you to sink, and others allow you to soar, even when you didn't know you had wings.

CHAPTER 26

RECOGNIZING SOUL FAMILY

What does it feel like to meet soul family? What does it feel like to meet a soulmate? What we are getting at is discernment of who and what is in alignment with you on a soul level. As the planet shifts, and as you shift, relationships that are not truly aligned on a soul level will no longer feel fulfilling to you. But we will remind you that you cannot discern what is of soul resonance from a place of ego or the mind. That is not vibrational discernment—that is thinking about it. To discern accurately requires that you are first centered within your heart, operating as your soul-self, seeing from a soul-led perspective, and already embodying the most authentic version of yourself.

If you are still caught up in illusions, if you are still projecting illusions, your process of "discernment" will look a bit different. You might be tuning into what is a match based on fear, conditioning, or familiarity instead of soul resonance. And so you must reset your barometer, so to speak, for full accuracy. If your speedometer at rest is already at 20 mph, you understand that the reading will be inaccurate, and so it is the same with discerning vibrational resonance. You must first calibrate yourself to your truest, most authentic soul frequency. You must first calibrate yourself to divine love. Those who skip this step will have trouble with discernment. Then set the intention to discern from your heart, from your soul—not your logical mind. When you are anchored into authenticity and when you are so familiar with your soul's voice, discernment is effortless. It is clear. You can simply tune into your soul knowing.

Now, when you meet someone who is truly aligned with your soul, who is soul family, or a soulmate, you will have a soul-knowing deep within. They might feel extra familiar, like you are picking up from somewhere you left off long ago, because your soul recognizes them. The familiarity is on a soul level. You recognize their vibration as an energetic match for your authentic soul frequency, or you are familiar with their frequency on a soul level, as opposed to familiarity based on what you have experienced before in this particular lifetime.

Here we will clarify different types of soul recognition. When you are operating as your soul-self and you sense familiarity, this is from your soul memory—a vast range of experiences. The familiarity could be the remembrance of a relationship from previous incarnations, or it could be from having a similar frequency overall. That is what you would perceive as your souls coming from the "same place"—this is the simplest way for us to describe it. Some of you might say, "we're made up of the same stuff." The feeling of "coming from the same place" could be a soul remembrance that your most frequent incarnation points were, in fact, the same or similar. In a field of flowers, you recognize the other tulips grown in your area of the garden. That feeling could also be the soul recognition that your energetic signatures are extremely close to the same—your frequency coding is very similar. If you are a color on the color wheel, your colors are close to the same.

What we will offer here, however, is that just because you have soul recognition with someone does not necessarily mean that you are meant to or required to have a close or long-term relationship with them in this lifetime. You might recognize someone on a soul level because you are of a similar vibration, or because you have had relationships with them in other incarnations, but it is possible that it is not necessarily an aligned relationship in this lifetime. It is key to stay clear in the truth of vibrational resonance in your present reality, and not just form a long-term relationship because there is a soul connection. Just because there is a soul connection does not necessarily mean the relationship is ideal or healthy for you currently or in this lifetime. And so, soul recognition does not necessarily mean that relationship is meant to be prominent in your life. It might very well be, and you will experience the feeling of picking up where you left off long ago, ease and flow in the connection. But it also might not be—it could be a remembrance, but if that person is not showing up aligned with divine love, embodying their truest, authentic frequency, then it might not be aligned for you in this incarnation. The contracts can be different in each lifetime.

It is key not to get caught up in soul connection as justification for staying in unhealthy relationships. You must honor the resonance in your now. We will distinguish this soul recognition from the soul resonance you experience when you are anchored into your essence as divine love and embodying your truest energetic frequency—fully living as your most authentic soul-self—and you connect with someone who is of the same frequency. This is the vibrational match that provides the greatest depth of connection, the feeling of oneness, where you simply understand each other, because you are quite literally on the same wavelength. When you clearly emit your unique authentic code, what comes to you is that of soul resonance, but you must be truly radiating out your soul's frequency for this to come to you. If you are not being your most authentic self, then what will resonate with your frequency will not be that of soul resonance. The key is this—remembrance and recognition are different from resonance. You might recognize someone on a soul level, but is their frequency resonant with your authentic, divine essence?

When you connect with another of true soul resonance, you will feel as though you simply understand each other without having to explain things. You will notice that telepathy is more effortless, because telepathy is simply about being on the same frequency, tuning into the same radio station, so to speak. As resonant souls, you are already one step ahead, because you are starting on the same frequency. You will feel naturally drawn to them, but you might also feel an intensity of emotion. How do you interpret an intensity of emotion? Some interpret intensity as frightening, as wrong, as bad, as something to avoid, which is why some push away those who are most expansive to them at first. Notice the intensity, and then get curious about its root. Is it from this lifetime or another? If from another lifetime, is it relevant here? If from this lifetime, what is the frequency of the root?

This is one reason why some lovers quarrel or "dislike" each other before coming to union—they are intense mirrors for each other. They are so similar that they see themselves looking back at each other. They feel an intensity of emotion they have not before, and they do not always know how to wrap their heads around it or interact with it. They feel "out of control" because the emotion is not something they chose, but rather something that swept over them like an ocean wave. Because of this intensity, sometimes you push them away at first. It all depends on how you interpret intensity. You could identify the same feeling as fear or as excitement, depending on your perception. We invite you to shift into curiosity. What does the intensity really mean? In which direction is the vibrational pull? Sometimes intense emotions are a no, but sometimes they are a resounding yes! Sometimes they are an intuitive redirection, and other times they are a glaring opportunity for expansion. You must tune into your heart, into your soul, for a clear answer in each situation.

The term "soul family" could be referring to the soul group you incarnated with, those you have experiences with in other incarnations, those who are from the same place, those of a similar frequency code, and/or those who you resonate with on a soul level. There is overlap between these. As we use this term here, we are referring to the overlap. If there is one rainbow made up of different colors, which are different frequencies within the same rainbow, those from the "same place" are those who would be the same color. The closer they are to the same shade as you, the closer the exact frequency, the closer the resonance. For example, yellow-orange and yellow-green will be slightly different, but will still resonate in their yellow-ness, while yellow-orange and yellow-orange will resonate moreso.

When you meet soul family, you will notice that things flow. You will feel at home. You will feel understood. You might notice that you more easily open up and feel safe to be vulnerable, because you know that you will be understood. You feel deeply seen. You feel the energy of unconditional love. You don't need words or a quantity of time to feel the strength of the energetic bond between you. It is simply a knowing of resonance. You will also feel empowered and safe to be your most authentic self. It is easy, because your inner knowing is confident that you will be accepted as all of you. You might notice you say things you usually wouldn't, you explore things you usually wouldn't, you naturally release judgments of yourself and others, and you feel lit up and inspired. You more effortlessly align with your authenticity. You more easily align with divine love. There is no space or desire for illusion. The resonance holds space for divine truth. This is the sign of resonance.

You will also notice that certain knowings, feelings, memories, and skills are unlocked when you unite with someone in your soul family, someone of soul resonance. These meetings are timed perfectly as to when it is time for you to open up your next packet of soul memory, as we will call it. You might notice that after spending time with someone of true soul resonance, you start to remember experiences from other incarnations. You might notice that more of your spiritual gifts turn on. You might notice that your intuition becomes clearer. You might notice that you understand yourself in a new way, a deeper way. You might notice that you manifest more effortlessly in your life without even trying. You might notice that new inspirations or excitements unlock for you. It is like you are better able to access more of yourself. This is because connecting with another of soul resonance is like a key that unlocks more of your code, that unlocks your next steps. This is why these relationships are so important at this time. This is why you are craving them at this time—it is your internal guidance directing you to what will support you in remembering more of yourself. It is the most efficient path to aligning with your purpose, living your purpose, and remembering your mission.

We will also add that there will be important people in your life who are not necessarily from your "soul family" as you might think of it now. From your orientation point, soul family can expand. Your relationships in this lifetime are a collection of relationships with those you have incarnated with before as well as new energies. We will note that from our perspective, they are not new, as time is its own perspective, but for the purposes of this conversation, you might perceive it as new. And so, you need not "look" for those who you have incarnated with before, as other energies will come through for you at this time, but what you will notice is that all significant relationships will need to be a true vibrational match for your authentic energetic signature in this life. If not, you will feel misaligned, symptoms might arise from this, and you will always be hungry for more.

You will find your clearest flow when you are spending most of your time and energy in connections that are a vibrational match, that are of soul resonance. If you are still yearning for more or feeling unsatisfied in your relationships, then it is important to reflect on, first, if that yearning is from your ego or your soul, and if you are truly calibrated to divine love or if you are still confusing love for obligation, addiction, or outsourcing your own needs. Reflect on where you might not be taking responsibility for your own frequency. If you are aligned with love and authenticity, and it is a soul yearning, then the next step would be to reflect on where you are not feeling fully seen or understood, on where you feel the vibrational mismatch, and open space to receive those who are a vibrational match. Remember that so many are also feeling the call to soul family. As much as you are seeking them, they are seeking you. Open yourself to be seen by those who are a vibrational match. It's not just about finding each other—you must also decide to let them in, if you want to be truly seen.

ACTIVATORS

Those of you who did choose to incarnate together at this time are finally coming together. This is the time that soul groups are meant to come together, to anchor in higher frequencies onto this planet, to pave the way for a new way of being. As you come together with other souls who are a vibrational match, codes are unlocked on the planet that activate divine love, and you are shifting the planet by coming into these relationships. This is how you anchor in light. And so, you can think of it as individual lights dispersed across a large field, each one a brief glimmer. But when they are all brought together side by side in a concentrated space, the light shines brightly. It is a force. This is the coming together of soul family.

You will also activate others in your soul group through coming into contact with them. When you are in highest alignment and living your truth, living as your most authentic self, part of the contract is to meet others in your soul group and energetically "wake them up." You need not do anything for this to happen, but you will start to see that after simply coming into energetic contact with the person, a series of energetic events is triggered, and things start to turn on for them. That might be spiritual gifts, that might be recognition of where their life is misaligned, that might be seeing the world from a completely different perspective, that might be having other interests, and so on. It is an energetic trigger that was perfectly designed to occur at exactly the right timing. Notice who those activators are for you, as well.

This is true of vibrational alignment of many sorts—there is a reason why some people are drawn to certain people and others not. They are drawn to who is an aligned activator for them. You'll start to understand how important it is to move beyond the 3D words that are being spoken, as the vibrational transmission is much more powerful. The vibrational transmission is what is really happening. One person might explain a concept to you and it barely resonates, while another person explains the same concept, but this time it rings true in your whole body and activates another level of inner knowing. This is because the frequency of what was transmitted through them was an energetic match for you. That is why it landed. Again, this is the power of vibrational resonance. It does not always make sense to the logical mind, the same way that attraction will not always make sense to the logical mind.

As you become more attuned to energy, you will notice that you are conscious of being attracted to energy instead of surface-level characteristics. The attraction will make less and less sense to your logical mind. Energy shifts perception. Perhaps you have an idea of specific physical traits you admire. Someone with those exact physical traits might waltz into your life, but you feel no resonance. Someone with the opposite physical traits might waltz into your life, and you feel a current of electricity supercharge your body. Which is more compelling? Listen to the energy. It is taking you places your mind does not understand. It is guiding you to what is better than what you could have ever planned. You might start to notice this within yourself—why you know when you need to create distance, why you are drawn to certain music or books or teachers but not others. It is not about someone being right or wrong, better than or worse than. It is simply neutral guidance in terms of energetic alignment.

You don't need to worry about what is "bad" or "good" or "right" or "wrong," as this is where you are staying in duality, where you are jumping to labels rather than anchoring into the neutrality of divine love. All you must do is anchor fully into love, truth, and integrity yourself, and then you know your barometer is set, and you follow the natural flow of what you're guided to. But if you're living in illusions, if you're lying to yourself, don't be surprised if "attraction" leads you to more of the same. It is through this process that you will start to see how people who didn't resonate with you before now do, as you peel back the illusions and step into your own truth and authenticity. From there, you see people differently. Expect the resonance to shift. Perception is based on vibration. Perception is based on conditioning. And so, as you peel back the layers of the stories, wipe the slate clean, and rewrite the stories so they are truly aligned with love, your perception shifts. This is a key first step before attracting in a long-term relationship, if you want to effortlessly attract those who are truly aligned on a soul level. It all begins with you. You are that powerful.

Notice where your feelings have not caught up to your mind, and where your mind has not caught up to your feelings. This is what confuses many of you—when you feel the disconnect between your mind and your feelings. And so, what is leading—your mind or your heart? Your soul knows information that your mind has yet to grasp, and this is where your mind has not caught up to your heart. Here you see how you cannot always make sense of what your heart knows to be true, because it is bigger than your mind. It is beyond logic. It is your inner knowing. Your inner knowing does not require justification that makes sense to the ego. It does not require a linear path to get there. Listen to your heart's wisdom.

You will also feel this when your heart has not caught up to your mind. Where are you letting your mind lead? This is where you get into situations that "make sense," situations that you think will fulfill you, situations that you think will allow you to feel the way you want to feel, but they do not. And so you wait. And wait. And wait. How long will you be waiting? Listen to your inner knowing over your mind. Choose love now! Where have you fallen in love with an illusion? Where are you letting the workings of your mind trick you into settling? We understand that it can feel disruptive and concerning when your mind has not caught up to your heart. This is where you worry—*how can this be? It doesn't make sense!* This is a beautiful space to notice your ego and your conditioning. What stories are coming up for you? What limiting beliefs? What expectations? What assumptions? Allow yourself to be in loving awareness of the expectations you have. Why do you think it is wrong or bad to feel these emotions? Why are you judging your intuition? Why are you judging your inner knowing? Why do you not trust yourself? Why do you not trust your heart?

We are not guiding you to any definite conclusions, but highlighting these interesting places to look. These are the places where you can learn more about yourself and your underlying expectations, where you can bring what was subconscious into conscious awareness, where you can see where you might have been unintentionally limiting yourself, where you can allow yourself to be surprised. Again, what you truly seek is often delivered in a way you never saw coming. If you did, would you be questioning it? If you did, wouldn't it already be here? Miracles are miracles because you don't see them coming. When it comes to vibrational resonance, when it comes to alignment with those who are meant to be on your path, there is something much bigger at play than your mind. Your soul is guiding you. Allow yourself to receive the gifts.

CHAPTER 28

HOW DO YOU KNOW?

How do you know when you love someone? Exploring this question will require orienting from a different space, for to answer this question from the current mindset of the collective would look different from answering this question from the lens of the reality you wish to be living in. For when you are living as a being of love, living with and from unconditional love, you do love all. It is coming from a place of love that you see the world, and so your relationships will look quite different. They will not be based on need, but rather a foundation of sovereignty, of wholeness, and of balance. This is how deeper relationships can be formed, because the recognition of resonance is based on the truth of vibration—it is a clear perception, as your unique energetic signature is so clearly expressed.

What we will say to meet you where you are at is to listen to your heart. As basic as that sounds, it is true. Listen to your inner knowing. When you are aligned with your soul and your intuition, you simply know. If you question your inner knowing, this is where you are disconnected from the voice of your soul. This is where you do not trust Source. How many of you do not listen to your heart? How many of you let your mind lead? How many of you decide you are in love based on what makes sense, expectations, assumptions, illusions, or stories you've built up in your head? How many mistake love for lust, or love for admiration, or love for intensity, or love for familiarity, or love for addiction, or love for comfortability, or love for the intense release of emotions when you are in an exciting situation? If you are confused about whether or not you are in love, then you are either too stuck in your mind and your ego, or you are not in love. When you tune into the voice of your soul, you know. But it requires surrendering logic and the ego to recognize that inner knowing. Use your logic and reason for equations that align with logic and reason. When it comes to matters of love, when it comes to discerning vibration, when it comes to emotion, this is where you tune into the wisdom of your heart.

We will tell you more about divine love. Love that is truly unconditional. Love that warms your soul and reminds you of your infinite worth. Love that is unconditionally safe and assuring. Love that opens your heart to loving yourself unconditionally. Love that holds you as you express your truest self. Love that empowers you and reminds you of your strength. Love that flows through you and activates the embodiment of your highest self. Love that cracks you open in the most beautiful ways, that cuts through illusion, that dissolves the masks, that breaks down your walls, that heals you, that inspires you, that illuminates you, that aligns you with truth itself.

The divine love that is available to you is not dependent on you being any certain way. It sees you directly, deeply, and purely. It dissolves illusion. It mirrors to you the truth of who you are and what is not in resonance with this frequency. For this reason, many fear it. Sometimes that fear is conscious, and sometimes that fear is subconscious. Once you know, you can't unknow. When you know how sweet it tastes, everything else is dull in comparison. When you know how good it feels, you will not settle for anything less. And then, what will have to change? And so, you find yourself in a position where you must decide between avoiding truth and unintentionally settling, or choosing a divine experience by facing truth. Feeling your emotions. Choosing divine love. It is a choice for you to make. It is a choice to embrace a different way of being. It is a choice to expand fully into your truth. It is a choice to live as your most authentic self. When you experience it, everything that is not resonant sticks out like a sore thumb.

And so, some fear divine love because they fear truth. Some fear divine love because they know it will highlight what in their life is ready to change. Some fear divine love because they are afraid to be seen. Some fear divine love because they are afraid to see and know themselves. Some fear divine love because they are afraid of the unknown. Some fear divine love because they have never experienced it before, and they have assumptions about what they have not yet experienced. Some fear divine love because they are afraid of the power of their emotions. Some fear divine love because they are afraid of their own divinity. And some fear divine love because they are afraid to be free. All of this is the ego, the logical mind, the conditioning. Your soul is always guiding you to love, because that is its truth. That is its resonance. Isn't it interesting how your ego can fear what your soul desires?

You might ask, *but is it fair to ask the same of another—to act as divine love?* Why not? Do you not see the divinity with them? Do you not see them as divine love? This is not asking for perfection. It is holding the space for them to step into their truth. There is the vibration of the dynamic overall, as well as other frequencies that flow in and out of the dynamic as you move through your human experience. But this is your opportunity to support each other in calibrating to a higher frequency of relating—to hold each other accountable to living as divine love. This is possible for all.

You can love in all sorts of ways, with all sorts of people. The knowing is in your heart, not your mind. It is clear as day. If you're wondering, that's not it. And is that not it because it's truly not it, or is that not it because you're afraid to let yourself feel it?

CHAPTER 29

YOUR DIVINE LIFE PARTNER

If what you're really asking yourself is, *how do I know if I've met my divine life partner?*, we have another answer. First, we will remind you to release the attachment of what it means to have a divine life partner. Are you already creating stories in your head about how long it should last, what it should look like, and what they will be like? This may or may not be in your highest alignment. Some of you will find yourselves aligned with one life partner for most of your lives, and others a number of partners over time. Your journey is unique to you, perfectly chosen for you to live out the experiences you must for your soul's highest evolution. It is when you detach from the how, and even the what, that you make space for it to come in. It's not a forcing, but a knowing that you feel drawn to a deeper commitment and exploration. That commitment to another person is actually choosing a deeper commitment to yourself. Your relationship with commitment is a reflection of your relationship with yourself and how you show up for yourself. The divine life partner that is for your highest alignment will mirror for you, will support you in expansion, will be an activator for your growth. This can play out in many ways. But where are you trying to figure it all out ahead of time?

This is something that blocks so many of you. So many are living so far in the potential future or in the past that they are not being in the present. The present is where you find the answers, by simply allowing. The present is where you receive the truth. You don't have to sort out what will happen next week or next month or next year. Getting so caught up in that might actually shift your now in a way that isn't fully authentic to how you feel. Be present. Be fully present in every experience and every relationship. This will make it clear to you when it is time to commit more deeply, and when perhaps it is time to follow different paths. We would like to make clear that this is not wrong or bad or a failure, but a beautiful graduation. The closing of a chapter. Everyone has different contracts. Some will have many committed partnerships, and others will have less. All experiences are beautiful!

But we will invite you to explore this—what if you shifted your relationship with commitment itself? What if you realized that commitment is simply a willingness to be fully present in every moment, to receive every moment, to see truth in every moment? Commitment is not binding—it is presence. It is simply commitment to yourself—a decision to live in truth. While the fear of commitment could be based on previous experiences, trying to avoid the past, expectations of what might happen, not wanting to be stuck, or a fear of missing out on something better, a fear of commitment, as we see it, is really an avoidance of self. An avoidance of being still and present in the current moment. Because in that presence, in fully receiving each moment, each lesson, and each reflection, you see yourself clearly. What would it look like for you to commit to yourself? To honor yourself? To love yourself? To feel your emotions? To see and know yourself? It is only in commitment, only in presence, that you can experience true connection, whether that lasts for a moment or a lifetime. Your commitments to other people and to experiences can always be updated and adjusted, but to live in the energy of commitment is to show up fully in every experience you have. This is to embody your wholeness.

For us to address the question of recognizing love more clearly, we must explain how the energetics of relationships are shifting at this time. This will be important in order for you to grasp a deeper understanding of where you are in attachment. Part of the block is that you have bought into the idea that everyone needs to have one divine life partner, and you might have an idea in your head about what the relationship will look like and how it will flow. But relationships will look quite different the more your frequency shifts and the more the vibration of the planet shifts. Orient yourself from a place of being fully embodied as your highest self, clear in your authentic energetic signature, fully energetically self-sufficient, completely balanced within yourself, feeling divine love within yourself, accessing that directly from Source, and understanding your essence as Source. From that place, it will be "easy" for you to have what you might consider now to be "high standards" (which, we will add, is a subjective judgment rooted in conditioning) because you are evaluating all relationships from a different perspective. You are fully sourced within yourself, and so you are not looking for relationships to fill you up or to complete you or to fix you.

The desire for a relationship is not coming from an energy of lack, scarcity, attachment, or codependency. Let that sink in.

From here, you can release expectation or obligation energy. Much of that expectation and obligation energy is connected to entrapment in a relationship to make sure that person A has an energetic resource, which is person B. But you don't require someone else to be your energetic resource when you source from yourself—when you source from Source itself. And so you might notice that some relationships are completed more quickly than has been normalized in your society, and others last much longer than is normalized in your society, because there is no longer a need for instant gratification, there isn't a wonder if the grass is always greener, and you are not operating from lack or ego. You have what you need from within yourself. The most fulfilling relationships will be those that mirror most clearly for you, supporting you in more deeply understanding yourself, as this is your direct connection to Source.

It is the relationships calibrated to divine love that anchor in the frequency of love—that which you crave—because this is living your truest frequency and floating in the energy of Source itself. Relationships that are not calibrated to the frequency of divine love, the frequency many of you will be so used to within yourself at this point, will not interest you at all. There will not be resonance. It is through understanding yourself so deeply as an "individual" who is an extension of Source, and reconnecting to the Source within— your essence of divine love that is within—that you are then able to move into relating to the collective and its members in a different way. The relationship will serve the collective because it will be based in love, and you will understand that staying in relationships that are out of alignment with divine love lowers the frequency of the overall collective, which is nonresonant for all. The more you anchor into your mission, it will be effortless for you to prioritize divine love over any addiction to drama, as that will no longer be resonant.

Because the barometer will change, it will become more and more important for you to tune into vibrational resonance rather than the mind. You will recognize that following the mind over the soul leaves you unsatisfied. We will reflect to you that it has become normalized to settle for less than your soul desires, and that is certainly not serving anyone at all! How would you feel to find out your partner felt like they were settling by being in a relationship with you— from a soul-aligned place, not that of ego? We continue to point this out because there is a difference. Much of what you think are emotions from a soul-aligned place are actually reactions from the ego. Discern this first before interpreting your emotions.

The divine life partner that you seek is available to you. They are also seeking you. You are craving deeper connection, and this is available to you! But you have to choose it, and you must notice anywhere that you are settling for less than what you truly desire on a soul level. You must first meet yourself deeply, see yourself, and know yourself as deeply as you desire another to. You must unpack where you believe what you want is not possible, where you believe it is hard to find, where you believe it is not available to you—this will become true. Your beliefs shape your reality.

Every relationship will have a different frequency, and when you meet your life partner, their frequency will be a vibrational match for yours. We want to be clear that this does not mean they will be exactly like you in every way. You will find people who are resonant with you on a soul level who are very similar to you, some who are extremely different from you, and some who are in between. Being a vibrational match on a soul level goes beyond likes, dislikes, hobbies, and even personality. And we want you to understand that someone who is a vibrational match now might not be in the future. As long as you are attached to the idea of the relationship lasting throughout your whole lifetime, you will feel as though you have failed if things change. If you change. If they change. But it is not a failure. What if it is part of the contract? Even two people in a beautiful partnership who are fully authentic and sovereign within themselves can sometimes choose to part ways because the contract is complete. There is a knowing that the lessons are complete, frequencies have shifted, what was resonant before no longer is, the dynamic is more stagnant than expansive, and there is something else to move into. From this perspective, you will start to see "breakups" differently.

What are your beliefs about what it means to complete a relationship? There has been much shame and guilt attached to the ending of relationships, and much of this is based in deep religious programming and tribal programming from when it was necessary to stay together for a lifetime in order to survive. It is time to expand past this, heal these wounds, and update the programming. This means choosing differently. What we wish to share is there is not a right or wrong flow of relationship in one's life. So much of the judgment, resistance, shame, guilt, and fear is because there is a deep fear of going against the grain, of other people's perceptions, of doing something "bad," of "failure"—but who defined that? Whose perception are you choosing for?

When you shift the norm, when you perceive from a place of divine love, you understand that it was not failure at all, but part of the process. Much of the anger and frustration that arises when relationships end is because you are comparing the end result to a path you were attached to in your head—a story—or a path that was normalized by society for a variety of reasons. But is that what is best for you? Is that your truth? Only your heart knows your truth. This is the truth of your soul, not the beliefs of the ego. In living your truth, some of you will have many partners throughout your lives, some will have one main divine life partner, and some will not have one significant divine life partner. Release your expectations, and you will find your happiness.

CHAPTER 30

CHOOSING TO BE READY

You might wonder, can people who spend most of their lives not in a romantic relationship truly be happy? First, it is when you are truly happy whether or not you are in a romantic relationship that relationship attraction will become effortless for you. We will also remind you that just because you are in a romantic relationship does not necessarily mean you are truly happy. Happiness and being in a romantic relationship are two different things. But to answer the question from the energy we know many of you ask this from—many are not, but there are some that are here to be, especially as more galactic DNA becomes reactivated and your physical bodies shift. Everyone has different contracts and different lessons to learn. That being said, a key aspect of your experience is connection, and how things are shifting right now is to shift into a higher frequency of connection. It is through connection you more deeply remember yourself as Source. It is through connection you are fully able to calibrate both the divine feminine and divine masculine aspects within, through giving and receiving, through supporting and being supported. It is through connection you are able to explore the depths of yourself, places you could not see without the mirror and without the experiences that are called forward when in connection with another.

If you do feel a deep craving within for greater connection, first make sure you are fulfilling that from yourself first. From there you will know what frequency needs to be matched and expanded upon in your relationships in order for you to hold this frequency. Your barometer is the divine love that flows through you from Source itself, through you as an extension of Source itself. And so, this relationship might feel different from what you are used to, if you are not used to aligning with the divine definition of love. If you are used to obligation and expectation energy. If you are used to drama, games, or instability in relationships. If you are used to compromising yourself to make a relationship work, or to make someone else feel better about themselves.

In a divine partnership, you will feel excited and encouraged to be all of yourself. To continue to explore all of yourself. To move and shift and grow. What many do not recognize in your current way of partnership is that committing to someone is also committing to honoring their expansion, not just to who they are in the moment. Committing to a relationship with someone is committing to honoring them and seeing them as the divine essence of love that they are, which means you must first honor yourself. Do you understand what it means to be in union with a multidimensional being? Where you resist this is also where you resist your own multidimensionality. And this will more prominently become an important piece of discerning who is an aligned long-term match for you and who is not.

We will point out, again, that the aligned partnership might feel different than you expect because it might be delivered in a way you didn't expect. Again, this is working beyond your mind, and it is also beyond the energy of drama and games that many of you are used to. Much of your dating world today is centered around games, drama, addiction to struggle, and looking to feel busy by producing illusions and stories. You choose to create this—staying stuck in cycles—when you are not ready for partnership. You choose to create this when you are not ready to set your ego aside and live from your soul, when you are not ready to allow yourself to receive love, when you are not ready to be truly seen, when you are not ready to release your addictions, when you are afraid of your own emotions, and when you are afraid of your own power. You are ready when you decide to be. When you truly decide you are ready, you will not require the games, the drama, the back and forth, and the unclear communication to keep you distracted. You will have no need to attract dynamics of that sort. The level of commitment, clarity, and respect that shows up in those you attract will mirror the level of commitment, clarity, and respect you have within yourself.

What if it was as clear as—is this a vibrational match or not? When you are not caught up in your own problem addiction, the sea doesn't have to feel so stormy. You will feel the ease, the grace, and the flow of attracting what you desire. What makes a partnership "difficult"? Is it difficult because you are trying to move through chronic resistance? That is a signal for you. Or is it "difficult" because it requires more of you? It requires all of you. It requires you to look at the places you are meant to look for your expansion. It requires you to open your heart. It requires your honesty and clarity. It requires listening. It requires speaking your truth. It requires facing truth. These are different types of difficult.

We caution against reaffirming the story that relationships are hard, and that marriages are hard. It depends on your definition of "hard." Remember, one person's reality does not have to be yours. But if you have decided that it must be hard and there must be conflict, then you will be expecting this, and unintentionally create, attract, or perceive more of this. Notice what your beliefs are about how it will feel and how it will look to be in a long-term romantic partnership. Ask yourself, where is that from? Your divine life partner will be your biggest supporter as you navigate the waters of life, as you continue to explore yourself. You each will be the container for each other to feel safe in your expansion. And your partner will also reflect for you, mirror for you, and offer you opportunities to see yourself in different ways, because certain dynamics only do come up in relation to others. That is part of why this playground of life was designed as such. This is part of the beauty of connecting with different souls, with different energies, with different types of people. This helps you learn so much more about yourself, about others, and about what you are truly looking for in relationships. How much would you learn if you only had one teacher throughout your life, compared to if you learned from twenty teachers? You can only learn so much from yourself through perceiving yourself as an individual. The others in your reality, who are also extensions of Source, are also aspects of you, and so you learn more about the human experience through everyone.

CHAPTER 31

THE DIVINE MASCULINE AND DIVINE FEMININE

In our discussion of attraction and relationships, we will move to polarity—a popular topic in your explorations of relationship dynamics. To understand both masculine and feminine energies within will be key for your personal expansion and growth and to learn to source from Source itself, from yourself, rather than externally. All of you have both masculine and feminine energies within you. It is these together that make up Source itself. It is both energies together that balance the one, that complete the circle, that together are everything that are wholeness. And so, you as a reflection of Source also have this balance within yourself. The collective overall has a balance between both. Remember, everything is energy, and energy flows in the way of achieving balance. When we say balance, feel into that energy instead of trying to understand it literally. The way "balance" plays out depends on the situation, but for the purposes of this transmission, explaining it in this way will help us move further with our discussion.

What you have felt for much time has been an intense imbalance related to masculine energy, leaning far in one direction, creating an underlying vibration of nonresonance, and so the divine feminine is stepping forward to bring things back into balance. What this means individually is understanding how these energies show up within yourself and in your relationships. And so, masculine energy is the energy of action, of doing, of structure and support. It is the container that holds the feminine, for without the masculine, without its stable boundaries, the beautiful force of the feminine has no direction in which to flow. Her magic is not fully harnessed. Masculine energy is the structure that allows the feminine to safely flow within. It is the clear edges that allow space for the softness. Feminine energy is the flow, it is intuition, it is the space of creation, it is empathy and compassion, it is receiving, it is resting, it is loving, it is flow state, it is the space of everything. It is the space of all creation. But what is there to create into without the masculine?

What we will point out is that over time the ego has taken over, and instead of embodying the divine forms of these energies, they have become twisted into their wounded and disempowered forms. And so, aggression, over-controlling, dominance, and tyranny have taken the place of loving, supportive structure, of safely holding and honoring the feminine. Guilt, shame, gullibility, low self-worth, and lack of trust have overshadowed the deep wisdom and magic in the essence of the divine feminine. This shift in modeling, this shift in energies, is what has disconnected you from your full power. As each of you identify these energies within and start to shift into their divine expressions, you re-access your power, and you source within yourself.

As all structures in your society represent these—and you have been "controlled" by the wounded masculine—the structures set up around you box you in, try to force you to be a certain way, and attempt to disconnect you from your intuition as much as possible so you do not question the status quo or those who have been in charge. This is draining your power. This is creating the illusion of separation from Source. And so, as you reunite within yourself and embody both the divine feminine and divine masculine energy within you, you reach your full power, your intuition, your own inherent structures, and you step out of codependency. If you subconsciously live in the belief that you require something outside of yourself for safety, for structure, and to provide, you will always be trapped in the systems that be, and you will always be dependent on something outside of you. This feeds those systems that trap you. Instead of living in the illusion that you must source externally, you learn to source from within. You source from the divine masculine and the divine feminine itself—the energy of the divine father and the divine mother themselves, which are simply aspects of Source, which you are an extension of.

It is this understanding that sets you free. It is this understanding that allows you to create a new way of being, because you remember the power of creation within yourself. You remember that the divine masculine within you is your structure and safety, that Source itself is your provider, that the divine feminine within you is your direct access to divine wisdom, through your intuition, which is your flow state, where you are in the stream of magic and miracles. You remember that Source itself is holding you with its compassion and endless love. And you are reconnected to the power within, from all angles.

This will also shift your barometer of attraction, and the expectations and assumptions within relationships. It is where you naturally move beyond roles that others have assigned to you—roles that have felt restricting for some time. You are moving into an age of authentic self expression—of truly loving interaction—that does not box anyone in. Rather, it honors everyone as a unique individual and a crucial aspect of the one. It allows space for everyone to be endlessly provided for and loved by being who they really are and doing what they genuinely love, what they are naturally gifted at, and what feels good for them. What would it look like for relationships to be without expectation, without attachment, and without assumption? We invite you to sit with this, and feel into any resistance.

The first step is to explore these energies within yourself, and to nurture the divine masculine and feminine within. To have healthy boundaries that are from divine love, to be clear with your intentions and take action in alignment with what you wish to create, to create healthy structure for yourself so your feminine energy has room to flow. To be in a state of flow and creation, to tune into your intuition, to get lost in your creativity, to love deeply, to rest. For without the divine masculine within, you will not feel safe to sink so deeply into love. Without the divine feminine within, you will feel disconnected from your emotions and intuition, and not fully feel the love available to you.

Many of you have felt disconnected from your emotions for a long time, hardened as a way to protect yourselves from the pain, never taught how to fully move through the depths of your emotions, how to manage this, or what it means. We understand that this has been part of your survival! Emotional pain hurts just as deeply, if not more, than physical pain. It is all energy, and the intensity comes through in different ways. We send so much love to you. And, now you might recognize that where you have hardened yourself to protect and numb yourself from the pain, you have also hardened yourself to fully experiencing love. Divine love will dissolve the shield, but only if you choose to receive it. Only if you choose to allow it.

There are many beautiful practices you can use to dissolve the shield. There are many methods of moving the energy through and learning to feel your emotions in a safe way, but what we will say broadly is that it is love that will dissolve the shield that holds you back. It is love that heals, at its core. Orient from love and watch what unfolds. And so it is love that can help you open your heart. Love from Source, from yourself, and through connection with another. This is a reminder of the warmth within. Love transmutes illusion. And you are here to experience divine love. For some of you, dissolving the shield is a very physical process. For some of you, the choice will be made quickly, and so it will dissolve quickly. Where have you chosen to put up the shield? What would it look like to put it down and open your heart?

CHAPTER 32

POLARITY

This comes back to developing your relationship with yourself. It is about trusting yourself. It is trusting the universe. Because when you trust yourself fully, and you are fully aligned with love within yourself, you can trust your inner guidance of when you are meant to open your heart and sink more deeply into a relationship, and perhaps when it is not the right time, place, or fit. You need not share all of your heart with everyone. The key is developing a clear knowing that is based in divine love as to when to open, when to receive, when to give, and when to not. Your energy is a beautiful, precious treasure, and you are responsible for who has what type of access to it. The divine feminine within will give you this intuitive nudge, and the divine masculine within will support you in setting healthy boundaries. That is not avoidance. That is not a barrier to never let anyone in, but a loving boundary—out of love for yourself and others. This coexists with unconditional love.

When you are fully aligned with these energies within, you will find that you are inspired, that you are expressive, and that you are energized. Much of your fatigue and physical symptoms actually come from an imbalance of these energies, like two generators that have been turned off for much time. Now it is time to turn them back on! It is in reconnecting with these divine energies, reconfiguring them, turning them on, living from them—however you wish to see it—that you have reconnected to the divinity within, to Source within. It is from here that you self-source. We will also remind you that this is the same as sourcing from love itself—an endless supply of "clean fuel" you will never run out of. Have you noticed that when you feel divine love, you feel as though you will never run out of energy?

From here, you can recalibrate to your natural state of flow. What is the balance that feels good for you between these energies? Everyone has a unique energetic signature, and in living authentically, they will have a different ideal balance of divine masculine and divine feminine within their systems. It is from finding this authentic balance of the divine masculine and divine feminine within that your authentic codes will be released and expressed clearly, and you will find attracting what is truly in alignment with you on a soul level becomes effortless, because now what is a vibrational match becomes clear. Remember, it is not something you have to figure out logically. It is something you be. You be your most authentic self, and everything else aligns. Most of you have been taught to show up in one way based on conditioning and modeling, but is that authentic for you? Or is that the conditioning? This is where your exhaustion and your dis-ease come from—from being inauthentic.

What many of you refer to as "the spark" in romantic relationships is the balance of polarity. This is where you create a balanced frequency within the consciousness of the relationship as a whole, which is its own essence. You might also find that some dynamics have a more masculine energy as a whole and others have a more feminine energy. We will remind you that this is separate from sex or gender. The more you understand yourself on a soul level, you will see and understand each other soul to soul in terms of resonance. It is beyond the physical body. And so, to deepen your understanding of energetic attraction, you will see that feminine energy and masculine energy are attracted to each other. The universe is seeking balance, and energy flows to come back into balance, but that does not mean it is never out of balance within a specific container in the process of finding balance once more. Energy flows. It is like a seesaw coming back into balance, or a pendulum swinging back and forth. This is true for you individually and within relationships. Within relationships, you will find a consistent dance and flow of both partners leading with both energies, where one partner holds space as the other deeply feels their emotions, and then vice versa. Within conversation, you feel this dance, as one speaks and the other listens.

At the same time, both are feeling, and both are holding the container. Because from a higher perspective, it is not one or the other—it is both. What we will also explore is, what if both are leaning into their feminine essence at the same time? The more you are fully sourced within yourself, sourcing from Source itself, you will actually step into something different in terms of relationships. To be clear, right now these understandings of polarity and balancing masculine and feminine energy in relationships are important steps to divine union and understanding sexual attraction. It is the balance of masculine and feminine energy that is one of the key factors which lights the spark for a sexual attraction rather than that of a friendship or other type of partnership. But as the frequency of the planet continues to shift, there will be an expansion of this understanding. There are new energies entering the field. There are beings beyond your planet that have a more masculine essence overall, and others with a more feminine essence overall, and some with both energies in equilibrium as their core essence.

There are souls incarnating on your planet now that hold different codes than have been activated on your planet before. As you step fully into sovereignty, this dance of polarity within relationships will also shift because you will be calibrating to equilibrium from Source itself, from the Source within, and will not feel so intensely when your partner, for example, leans more into their feminine or masculine essence. And so, if both partners are holding the feminine, it will not feel the same as it might have before. It will not feel as ungrounded, because both are still held, but the experience will be different overall. As time goes on, you might find there are more beings incarnated than there are at the time of this transmission that don't lean more in one direction than another in terms of masculine and feminine energy, but that feel balanced authentically. Everyone's unique code is different. And so, for those essences, they might not lean so far in either direction, and the balance might be the same for those in relationship.

We point this out because it is important for you to lean into your authenticity, not what someone else is telling you is your unique energetic code. Only you know this. But you can only discover this if you try it out for yourself and feel into your internal knowing of what is authentic. Spend time in your divine masculine, and time in your divine feminine. We say this, but really you are always embodying both—it is really just where you are leaning in the moment, and how you are acting or being. Try out different ways of moving through the world, different rhythms, and leaning far into both. These experiments will help you come back into balance yourself. This might also shift with the seasons!

This time is about breaking out of structures, out of "shoulds," out of the way you have been told it must be. You are moving into an age of true authenticity, of true uniqueness. You feel this as people are breaking norms—they are testing the waters, exploring their inner desires and knowing that there is something more for them, something else that wants to move through them. But if you are depending on someone externally to be your divine masculine or divine feminine, you are still in dependence when you need not be. These are sourced from within you. These are sourced from Source itself. And when you come to the place where you are truly your most authentic self, you might find that your most authentic expression is leading more with your feminine energy, or leading more with your masculine energy, or an equal amount of both. Attraction will shift based on this, which is why living your truth first is the way to effortlessly magnetize what is in highest alignment for you now.

You might wonder, if like attracts like, then why would feminine energy attract masculine energy? And so, this is where romantic attraction becomes even more interesting, because what you will come to find is that you are romantically drawn to souls that are of a similar frequency, but lean into the "opposite" in terms of masculine and feminine energy, because the natural state of the universe is to find balance, and this creates balance in the overall frequency of the relationship, and this is what ignites "the spark" within you. This is where you might feel as though someone "completes" you. They are not completing you, but rather the energy of the relationship dynamic itself, the consciousness of the relationship. You have the feeling of a complete whole because the energy of the relationship is balanced, not leaning off to one side.

There is also attraction to those of the same pole. Think of feminine essences who are drawn to other feminine essences, and same with that of the masculine. These relationships are also beautiful and deep, but in their own way. Two beings that come together who are both more naturally in their feminine energy, based on their authentic code, and showing up in the relationship in that divine feminine energy can deeply honor and love each other, and likewise with that of the masculine, but this is a different type of attraction. Romantic attraction mirrors sexual energy, mirrors creation itself, which is the coming together of the masculine and feminine energy to create the whole, to create balance. We remind you—this is separate from sex and gender. Anyone of any sex or gender can authentically have more of a masculine essence, feminine essence, or resonate equally with both. This is why sexual attraction is outside of sex or gender—which are unique to this incarnation and not relevant in all dimensions. Remember, your soul does not have a sex or gender. You will start to see far beyond this.

We will give an example of how these energies might balance. Perhaps you start with person A who, according to their authentic code, naturally vibrates at 70% feminine energy and 30% masculine energy in this expression, moving through the world in this way, most aligned. And for the romantic, sexual relationship essence to feel balanced, in terms of the overall underlying vibration—the relationship's energetic signature—the romantic attraction will stabilize with person B, who naturally authentically vibrates at 30% feminine energy and 70% masculine energy. As either person shifts, then the other will either shift or will not, and here you see where resonance continues or it does not. What authentically recalibrates in alignment, and what becomes nonresonant, will depend on the situation.

Again, we will remind you—throughout all relationships, each individual shifts in terms of leading with their masculine or feminine energy, depending on the moment and situation. We also want to clarify—you come into energetic harmony and activate your full power when you have equally and fully embodied both your divine masculine and divine feminine energies. Part of this is healing any wounded or distorted versions of each of these energies, and then integrating and applying these divine energies in your life. When you have restored your full divine feminine energy and full divine masculine energy, it will feel like having "equal access" as opposed to one energy feeling more difficult to utilize or lean into than the other. And, while you have that "equal access" and inner balance, you reach inner union. These energies are able to work together to keep you vibrationally aligned. From there, according to your unique energetic code in this lifetime, you might find that you naturally lead from one of those energies more than the other. You are still balanced in this state, because you have the foundation of fully activated and embodied divine feminine and divine masculine energies available to you at all times.

To give another example, there might be person A who vibrates at 50% feminine energy and 50% masculine energy, who then attracts someone of the same balance, romantically. This will be a different type of relationship for many to understand, as your teachings of polarity will need to be expanded upon. The polarity in a relationship is, at its core, about each individual being fully integrated in both their divine masculine and divine feminine energies, and able to dance with the other in the relationship, swapping back and forth between who is holding which pole in which moment, in order to maintain energetic balance, support, and polarity in the relationship. More of these equally balanced beings are coming to your planet and more equally balanced energies are being activated on your planet at this time—offering a new example of being and relating. The higher the frequency, the more balanced the energies will be, in terms of embodiment. You will lead from both. This is not better than or worse than, it is just vibration, soul evolution, and energetic signature. As your frequency shifts, the energetic dynamics that feel most aligned will also shift.

CHAPTER 33

SOULMATE CONNECTIONS

We will deepen our discussion by exploring different types of relationship connections, including soulmates, karmic soulmates, and twin flames. These terms are used regularly, and not necessarily in the way that we will refer to them here. We will explain these terms as we will use them in this transmission. We will also add that it is a common trap to attach to one of these labels and to get too caught up in the label, and this might point to where you are still in attachment, still in seeking rather than attracting, and not trusting your soul.

When you are curious about the type of connection, you will simply know the truth in your heart. But you also do not need a label to understand it. You will feel the vibration. You will know. It will reveal itself. It will reveal itself whether or not you have a label for it. Allow it to unravel, and enjoy the experience! What we will caution against is using a label to justify staying in a relationship that is not aligned with love. Someone being your soulmate, karmic soulmate, or twin flame is separate from whether or not they are an ideal match for you in a relationship right now. You must honor the truth of the now. What is the current frequency of the dynamic itself? Is it aligned with your highest frequency?

Soulmates, as we define them, are not a single person. By this we mean you do not have just one soulmate. You have many soulmates. In fact, when you live as your most authentic self, your reality will recalibrate so everyone in your life is some type of soulmate. The idea of "the one" in your society has come from an experience of what we will explain as twin flames, and the concept becomes confused. People spend their whole lives looking for their other half, living in a story, looking for a potential, living in the energy of separation, and it is, unfortunately, based on a large misconception. It is one manifestation of giving your power away, and forgetting your wholeness. We understand the appeal of the illusion—that you must simply find that one person and suddenly all your problems are solved. If anything, they would be highlighted!

Everyone has different contracts and experiences, and there is not just one person who will be an ideal relationship partner for you. We will remind you that you have free will. You have many different timelines to choose from. There is an interplay between contracts, what you might call destiny, and free will. When it comes to your relationship experiences, each relationship has a slightly different frequency because it is a different mixture of energetic signatures. They are all different, but there will be some that feel authentic to you, and others that do not, and ones that feel authentic to different parts of you, and some that feel authentic to different timelines. And so, understand that you are choosing timelines. If it is vital in this incarnation for you to meet someone specific, it will occur, and there are different timelines for this to occur—different entry points.

What is interesting is that many of you crave the liberation of choice, yet you also fear it. You stay paralyzed knowing that you choose the timeline. You wonder, *what if I am making the wrong choice?* You can't make the wrong choice. There are no wrong choices. Many of you are trying to understand relationships and love from the perspective of what is right, what is wrong, what is better, and what is worse. You wish to put it in a formula. Love is not a formula. When it comes to matters of divine love, there isn't an objective right, wrong, better, or worse. There might be situations that feel "right" for you, and feel "better" for you—but this is your interpretation of vibrational resonance. If you are looking for an understanding of love the same way you are looking for the right answer to a math equation, this is where you are resisting your intuition, and not trusting yourself.

Trust yourself! There is no "wrong" choice. You are simply choosing different experiences. And if you choose one experience, but it is crucial for you to have a different one according to your soul contracts, you will be led there one way or another. Remember, you can always make different choices, if you so choose. Commitments can change. When it comes to making the most aligned choices for you, you must tune into your highest truth at that moment. The choices that will feel most resonant for you will feel like flow to your soul, will be based in divine love, and will be those that honor your truth and authenticity. We will point out that sometimes the most resonant relationships for your soul are terrifying to your ego. Listen to your soul. And so, some relationships will feel more resonant than others, but timelines intersect in many places, and you can always make different choices.

What feels authentic to you now? What is your truth now, anchoring into your highest alignment and authenticity? What is the choice from a place of divine love right now? That is all you need to know to align to your highest timeline! From there, move forward with detachment from a particular outcome or how it must look. Be open to the energy flowing in whatever way it needs to. And so, if you wish to align with a soulmate, all you must do is make sure that you are clearly expressing your soul's unique code, and living your truth. Live from the voice of your soul, and watch what happens. Soulmates can come through in a variety of ways. These are souls that you have deep connection and resonance with. These are souls that you have incarnated with previously. These are souls that are from the same part of the frequency bandwidth as you. These are souls that have a similar vibration. These are souls that are the same note in the song. They are the same color in the rainbow. Soulmates can be dear friends, parents, siblings, teachers, lovers. You will meet more than one soulmate in your life, and these relationships will feel like home, in a peaceful, loving way. You have known this frequency for a very long time.

And so, you do not just have one soulmate, and they can come through in different ways. This is also not to say that your divine life partner must be a soulmate connection in the sense of someone you have spent many lifetimes with already, because there are also incarnations where you are meant to connect with new energies, different frequencies, and mix more colors of the rainbow, so to speak. However, you will still have that feeling of resonance, because you are meant to spend lifetimes together. You are feeling the "future" that has yet to occur. We are explaining this within your orientation point of past, present, and future for ease of communication, but we will remind you that from another dimensional perspective, it is all occurring at once.

Again, the resonance will naturally align when you live authentically and release your own limitations, expectations, and judgments, and watch who comes into your life and aligns with the frequency of divine love that flows through you. Not all soulmate connections will be prominent relationships in your life forever. Some might be prominent only for a short time, while others might be for a long time. The length of the relationship in this incarnation does not indicate the impact. Not all soulmate relationships will be healthy for you in this lifetime, and so you must honor this truth.

But when you do connect with a soulmate energy, and you are both living in alignment with your truth and authenticity, aligned with the path of divine love, you will find that these relationships are some of the most stable, loving relationships you will ever come across. There is a deep sense of loyalty, trust, and safety, because you have done this before! You know each other on a soul level. This is one way in which soulmate connections can mirror for you more deeply—they have already been with you for other layers of your experiences as a soul. The same way a friend who has known you all your life can tell exactly how you feel with a moment's glance, while a new friend might not be able to read between the lines quite as quickly and needs more time to catch up, a soulmate connection can jump into depth more quickly and can powerfully mirror for you more quickly. Soulmate connections can also mirror quite powerfully because of your similarities. When one has uncovered, deeply explored, and healed a part of themselves, they will more easily recognize that in others.

You might also find that aspects of your relationship with that soulmate in other incarnations will come forward again in this experience, and these are opportunities for deeper understanding, for deeper healing, for clearing of old energies, for faster leaps into new ones. If you have been practicing with a dance partner for years, you will more easily sync your steps on the dance floor than if you dance with a new partner. When the frequencies are similar, you will see more of yourself in that other, and here you will find a clearer mirror for you. If you have a lifetime of experience dancing in a particular style and are wishing for deeper mastery, would an ideal teacher, mirror, guide, or partner not have a lifetime of experience with the same? Remember, you do not need to try to find soulmates. When you embody your authenticity, they will come into your field. In fact, most of you are already aligned with or at least around soulmates, whether or not you have already recognized them as such. You already decided to connect. You will find that the more and more you align with your authenticity and truth, you feel that everyone around you is a soulmate, because your reality will recalibrate to only soulmate connections. There is a deep sense of knowing and connection. It is easier to open up. It is like you're made up of the same stuff!

What we would like to unravel is the idea that relationships require time to be developed. Some relationships will take longer to unfold. In some relationships, it will take longer for love to grow (or rather, to be consciously felt), and in others it will happen more quickly. There is no right or wrong, better or worse, as we wish to invite you to see beyond that perspective. It will depend on the circumstance. It will depend on how connected each individual is to their soul's voice. It will depend on how well each person knows themselves on a deep level. It will depend on how much they have learned from their previous relationships. It will depend on their ability to discern. It will depend on what feels authentic for them. It will depend on the contract. It will depend on your choices!

There is a trend in your society that the most "successful" relationships—according to your general definition, referring to the relationship lasting and the partners continuing to feel love—often have a slower beginning. Yet, you also know of old couples who simply knew immediately! Everyone's contracts are different. We will point out that the slower beginnings can allow for more time to ensure that you are evaluating from your soul rather than your ego, that you can get to know the different layers of the person and their truest self, that you can sort through what is your soul, what is your mind, what is your logic, what your emotions are, and what they mean, and that you can get out of your own way when it comes to expectation and attachment. But for those who are not in attachment, expectation, and assumptions, for those who truly know the voice of their soul, for those who have developed the skill of discernment, for those who trust themselves, for those who do not let their mind get in the way, for those who are living their authenticity and truth and know how to identify vibrational resonance, they do not necessarily need much time to know. They will simply know. But you must be honest about if you are truly at that point or not. If you are still living in any illusions with yourself, if you do not know the depths of yourself, then you will still be perceiving from this lens. But as more of you truly live from your soul and learn to trust your intuition, you will not need much time to accurately discern what is a match and what is not—you will just know.

The inaccuracy is a result of the barometer being off, of the discernment being unclear, of where you might have been orienting from ego rather than soul. This is not worse or bad—it is simply being honest about how accurate your barometer is when it comes to guiding you from your soul. The more you know yourself, the more you know your own frequency deeply and clearly, of course it will be easy for you to spot its match! It is a song you've heard a million times. You have every word memorized, every note, and every beat, and you don't even have to think about it. Your ability to discern soul matches quickly is simply dependent on how well you know yourself.

CHAPTER 34

KARMIC CONNECTIONS

You might also encounter souls you feel a karmic connection with. In these connections, there is something to be completed or rebalanced from another incarnation. You will feel a strong draw to someone you have a karmic connection with, and you will often experience intense synchronicities that bring you together. This is because there is some type of contract to be completed or energies that need to be rebalanced, and so divine orchestration will ensure you come together for an opportunity for things to be healed, cleared, and put back into balance. These karmic connections can sometimes feel quite intense, depending on how they play out and what energies need to be rebalanced. For example, you might find that someone is contracted to help you in a profound way because you played that role for them in another incarnation, or because they did the opposite in another incarnation. You might find that a relationship that did not end very well is revisited for you both to show up from a higher frequency and clear the energy. If there is an energetic "debt," so to speak, that must be paid, there will be an opportunity for this to be done, but there is also the chance one or both of you do not choose to repay this debt or show up differently. You have choice. Although we will point out, sometimes it can feel as though you don't, simply because the energy is pushing you so strongly in a certain direction!

The rebalance comes when you meet the situation from a healed, empowered, whole place—from an energy of divine love. The same way you will continue to attract similar dynamics in different relationships in this lifetime until you learn the lessons required to shift the energy and attract in something different, you will see this across incarnations. The intensity in karmic relationships comes from a few different factors, including the rich history between the souls, the intense recognition, the soul remembrance of the intense emotions, as well as the fact that these karmic relationships are often connected to your deepest wounds and biggest lessons. They are some of your greatest opportunities to raise your frequency, and to heal and clear energies on a soul level. You will feel the shift on a soul level.

Despite popular belief, not all karmic relationships are difficult or intense. Some of the people you are closest with in your life are most likely karmic soulmates. Balancing energy and learning your biggest lessons are not always hard, difficult, or low-frequency experiences for you. That being said, other karmic relationships are extremely triggering. Sometimes the connections are triggering because the patterns and dynamics between you are genuinely unhealthy, like being out of integrity and dishonest with each other. Other times, these relationships are triggering because of the deep wounds they touch. For those who have not yet learned to deal with triggers from a curious, empowered place, this can lead to intense arguments, low-frequency emotions and decisions, and so on. One who is in alignment with their soul frequency and who is anchored in divine love will receive "triggers" differently, and will perceive karmic connections differently. Again, the perception and the reaction will shift as the frequency shifts.

When it comes to karmic connections, these energies will continue to play out until the energy is balanced out, the lessons are learned, one or both of you has recalibrated, or the "debt" is repaid. We don't recommend the word debt because of its connotations—this is not about "owing"—but it gets across the point of balanced energy. Harmony. Realignment with divine love. We will add that at the time of this transmission, many of these karmic contracts are completing, as the energy is getting fully balanced. Remember, while you cannot control another, as they have free will, you can control how you respond, how you show up, and what frequency you hold. You need not worry about the other person's side of the vibrational bargain. Simply take responsibility for your own. There is always a lesson— an opportunity for growth and expansion—on your side, as well. When you complete your side of the contract, you shift the energy for yourself. Your soul is guiding you to energetic balance and inner harmony. Your soul is guiding you to the places that need to be looked at and shifted in order for you to align fully with divine love and your truest expression. This is why the intensity of these connections is so distinct—it is an intense draw that many of you would find impossible to ignore. It is pulling you to cycles that need to be completed. It is shining a bright light on where there is unfinished business.

As you are on the path of attracting your ideal life partner, your best friend, or a relationship of any sort, part of the process of becoming energetically and vibrationally available for that person will be to attract in relationships that allow you to clear up any energetic imbalances and finish any unfinished business that must be completed for you to move to the next level of the game, where your next most aligned match is. It is a crucial part of the process. When you take the opportunity to balance the energy, to show up with divine love, as divine love, to show up from an empowered place of love, to not continue to feed the old cycles, to not fall into the disempowered patterns, to not fall back into lower frequencies, you will notice a massive shift in your vibration on the other side. These are the super boosts in your video game!

As you learn to meet people consciously, with open eyes and an open heart, and you understand that you are a multidimensional being, you will start to recognize why you are so intensely drawn to or repelled by certain people. Notice which connections are natural. You pass by people every day and don't necessarily pay attention to all of them. Why is this? Why do your eyes naturally meet some people's, yet not others? Why do you notice a certain person in a sea of people, but not others? Frequency, vibrational resonance, and contracts. When there is a contract to be fulfilled, your souls will be brought together.

When you come into contact with that energy again, your soul memory is triggered, and this is why you might feel an intense emotion that doesn't seem to have a logical response, such as deep love for someone you just met or deep mistrust of someone you barely know. Sometimes this is an intuitive awareness of what is occurring in this lifetime, and other times it is soul memory. Notice where the energy is very intense, and tune into your soul memory as to why. If you felt betrayed by someone in a different reality, and you just met them in this one, you might immediately feel repulsed even if your logical mind doesn't recognize why. We will add that just because you experience them as untrustworthy in another reality doesn't mean you will in this one.

And so, you start to see how energetics become more complicated. You receive information with your 3D senses and your intuitive senses. You feel cellular memory and soul memory. You are drawn to or away from certain people, places, and situations based on what has happened in this reality, conditioning, where your soul is guiding you, and other experiences of the soul that might not be a part of this incarnation. These are all parts of you. For example, you might have an extreme phobia based on soul memory from a negative experience in a different lifetime, or a deep interest in a particular topic because that was your life's work in a different incarnation. Notice what you are drawn to and what you are repelled by. It is not random. Nothing is coincidence. This is where your soul memory comes online. You support the energetic equilibrium and frequency of your soul's expression overall when you heal and clear any relevant energies in this lifetime, because this also heals and clears the energies in other times, in other incarnations, and in other dimensions. The "you" now can shift the frequency and can heal a pattern felt by the you as a child. Remember, you are a multidimensional being.

So, with karmic relationships, there is unfinished business, and there is intensity, whether that is perceived to be positive or negative. These are souls you have had other expressions with, and so there is a deep understanding and familiarity on a soul level. Telepathy will be much clearer because of this, as it will be with soulmates that are not necessarily karmic, and soul memory will be clearer. You might notice you have stronger intuition around or related to these people. There are lessons here. There are lessons in giving, or receiving, or speaking your truth, or fully being yourself, or acting from love instead of fear or anger or guilt in these karmic connections. They reveal themselves in divine timing because you are ready for the energies to be rebalanced. When you avoid these lessons, they will come back around whether in this incarnation or the next. You will notice this to be true with the particular person involved—it is why they are still in your dreams, it is why you can't get them out of your head, it is why you keep hearing their name, or perhaps it is why you keep running into them. Your reality is going to show you what needs to be looked at! When a lesson must be learned, you will not escape it, no matter how hard your ego tries.

The path to the highest expression of divine love for you in this lifetime will be in learning the lessons in these karmic relationships. We will point this out again, because it is so key—each relationship you have, of every type, is preparing you. It is a necessary step. Many of you want to simply jump to the end result, but there is no end result. What you might think of as the end result is already there if it is meant to be. And so, every experience you encounter when you have aligned with your highest intentions is getting you there and teaching you everything you need to know for you to shift into the version of yourself where what you desire is already part of your reality. Can you allow yourself to enjoy this experience? You need not worry about where you are going. Be fully present in your now, or you might miss the lessons that are allowing you to become a vibrational match for what you desire! You might think you are "ready" when you are not yet a vibrational match, and so your soul guides you to the experiences, the lessons, the insights, the teachers, the people who will aid in your shifts so that you are a vibrational match. Embrace this process. It is, in fact, the most efficient way to bring your desires into your current reality.

Karmic relationships that express as romantic relationships are the ones where so many of you forget your energetic resilience. What we mean by this is that these relationships often involve an energy that you might refer to as "temptation," in that they tempt you to lower your vibration, to forget your boundaries, to act from lust or obligation or addiction rather than divine love for yourself. If both parties are not ready to choose to clear and balance the energy, these often manifest as relationships with patterns that might be considered toxic or unhealthy—push and pull dynamics, guilt trips, shaming, judgment, lack of boundaries, acting from a place of low self-worth or self-respect, dishonoring each other, and so on. This occurs for the same reason that so many of you do not stand firm in your own boundaries and energetic requirements when it comes to friends—you have deep love for someone on a soul level, and you think enabling them to act from their ego is love simply because it is easier, because it makes them comfortable. As we have covered, this is not love. It is of highest love for that other to act from highest love for yourself, and to hold them to the standard of divine love, as this is their truest essence. This is seeing them as love, from love.

This becomes especially relevant in romantic relationships. You might feel a deep soul connection, you might have a very strong spiritual connection with this person, you might experience many synchronicities related to them, you're intensely drawn to them, and you can't get them out of your head, yet when you look at the reality of how they are showing up—is it in alignment with divine love? You cannot allow your soul memory to confuse your perception. Many will blame their intuition, believing that if they are so intensely drawn to this person, if they love them so deeply, then it must be the right fit, and perhaps they will change, even if they are not showing up in alignment with divine love in the now. It was your intuition that drew you together for the lessons, not necessarily to stay in the relationship for any particular length of time.

Just because your intuition guided you to something that you perceive to have "not worked out" does not mean your intuition was wrong. Much of what you perceive to have "not worked out" we would argue worked out exactly as it was meant to. It brought you to the experiences and lessons necessary for your highest growth and evolution. Just because you interpret something as an experience you did not enjoy does not mean it was not meant to be part of the journey, although you might not see it that way in the moment. Life is a collection of experiences that invoke a range of emotions, and the lessons that are for your highest expansion will encourage you to meet the full range of those emotions. From the lowest lows, you will also propel into the highest highs.

To complete the discussion of karmic relationships, our point is to not have any expectations or assumptions as to how it will work out. Both people will choose what they will. There are instances where the energies are balanced, the patterns healed and cleared, you both choose to show up aligned with divine love, and then you enjoy a long, loving relationship. There are instances where the energies are balanced, the patterns healed and cleared, you both choose to show up aligned with divine love, and that completes the relationship—that's all there was. There are instances where the energies are left imbalanced, the patterns are not healed and cleared on both sides, you did not both choose to show up aligned with divine love, and the relationship might continue, or it might not. If it continues, it is inherently not supported with a foundation of divine love. If it does not, then the energy will return again at another time, in this incarnation or the next, for the next opportunity for whomever did not fulfill the contract.

CHAPTER 35

TWIN FLAMES

From here we will move to the concept of twin flames, noting that many who meet a karmic connection will confuse this for a twin flame connection. The term "twin flame" is used commonly in your society, and we will be clear about how we define this. A twin flame connection, as we define it, is a very specific type of soul connection that is quite uncommon to experience in your incarnation. There are not many twin flames incarnated compared to your overall population. A twin flame is a different type of soul connection than a soulmate, although many use the term "twin flame" when they are really referring to a soulmate. Many who are referring to their partnerships as a twin flame partnership at this time are not, which is why we suggest practicing discernment with all information you come across. You could consider a twin flame to be a type of soulmate, but not every soulmate is a twin flame.

There is a masculine and feminine aspect of each of you, and your soul is expressed in different realities all at the same time. When you move beyond your third dimension, you start to understand that your soul is everywhere. Your understanding of, and how you relate to, the concept of "twin flame" will depend on the dimension you are orienting yourself from. For this discussion, we are orienting from a dimension where you have the concept of an "individual" soul. From that orientation point, a twin flame is a soul that has incarnated in more than one body in the same time-space reality. In a split-soul twin flame dynamic, the divine feminine and divine masculine energies split into separate physical vessels to anchor in more light, to learn specific lessons, and to understand themselves more deeply, amongst other reasons. In other words, one soul will be expressed in two different bodies in the same reality.

This can also occur in a monadic twin flame dynamic, which is when the same exact soul frequency is incarnated in more than one body in the same reality, but the masculine and feminine aspects are not "split." Monadic twin flames have different energetic dynamics with each other than split-soul twin flames, and the key piece of their mission is not necessarily related to shifting relationship templates as it is with split-soul twin flames. When you have the same soul frequency in more than one body, the energetic laws of attraction will pull those frequencies together—resonant vibrations find each other. Twin flames are an exact vibrational match. However, the split-soul dynamic creates another energetic layer that might be felt like a balancing act—more of a push-pull dynamic, which we will explain further. This is part of split-soul twin flames' experience in their process of being the examples on this planet of internal masculine-feminine energetic dynamics, inner union, and updated relationship templates. For the purposes of our discussion, we will focus on split-soul twin flames, because it is the split-soul twin flame dynamic that mirrors personal and relationship energetics particularly relevant for all incarnated here—twin flame or not. But, it is important to understand that this is not the only twin flame dynamic, and all that we share below does not necessarily apply to monadic twin flames. We will move forward with our exploration of split-soul twin flames.

For those with an incarnated twin flame, their most important life lessons will be about relationships, will be about integration, will be in collaboration, will be in surrender, will be in releasing control, will be in seeing all of themselves, will be about loving themselves, will be about learning the depths of unconditional love. It is from different expressions of the twin flame dynamic that much of your messaging around "finding your other half" derives. These unions have an intensity beyond what many could imagine. One aspect of this intensity is because meeting an exact mirror, an exact soul frequency match, highlights and amplifies literally every aspect of you. This is different from soulmate mirroring. Another component of the intensity of this union is because there is so much energy to be anchored onto the planet, in fact, that the different aspects must split into two bodies. This also allows for a broader range of experience for the soul, a clear example of how one soul can be expressed quite differently, but where there will be uncanny similarities in expressions.

The twin flame experience allows for some of the most intense experiences of mirroring. When one soul is incarnated in two different bodies within one reality, there is the experience of meeting your soul directly, face to face, and looking at yourself so clearly in another physical form. In coming together, it is a uniting with the self. It requires you to see all of yourself and to know all of yourself. There is no hiding.

But it is the feeling of "missing" someone else throughout one's life that drives people to searching for that other part of them, and it is this union that has been played out in much of your media, has informed much of your rhetoric about relationships, and has confused many in what they will feel when they encounter their most aligned life partners. There are many different experiences available. But it is from the experiences of twin flames that many have believed there should be an intense push-and-pull energy or an explosion of energy upon meeting their divine life partner, when in fact for most of you, uniting with a soulmate will immediately feel comforting, loving, and calm. But in many types of connections, not just that of twin flames, you will feel an ignition of energy within you! This is your intuition. This is your body's wisdom. This is your body telling you to pay attention. This is the power of aligned energies coming into play—it does not matter whether or not the connection can be labeled, or what that label would be.

Being able to recognize a twin flame connection is not relevant for most of you as we see it, because the dynamic is going to play out whether or not you have a label for it. But we wish to discuss the topic further because there are so many of you who cling to the concept and create unnecessary attachment that in fact deflects your true soul desires. What we will say above all else is that when you dissolve expectations, assumptions, and logic, and instead tap into your authenticity, you don't need to understand labels. There are no rules! Remember, your beliefs create your reality. If your ego has decided that something has to happen as part of a certain romantic connection, such as feeling a certain feeling the second you meet your life partner, it can create a self-fulfilling prophecy that might lead you to something you did not in fact truly desire. If you have decided that a certain signal or feeling means someone is the one, then you will be looking for that—but what if that is from your mind rather than your highest truth? The twin flame journey can look different in each connection, although there will be common themes. The soulmate journey will look different for everyone. The divine life partner journey will look different for everyone. The journey of relationships will look different for everyone.

This is where we will remind you to be specific with what you are calling in, and also nonspecific. What we mean by this is to be clear in what you actually desire in terms of how you wish to feel, the vibration you wish to be anchored into, and how you are looking to expand into more of yourself through the connection. From there, release the expectations or assumptions about how and when it is meant to be delivered. This is about aligning with your soul-led desires rather than the wants of your ego. If you are spending your whole life looking for a twin flame, but you do not have one incarnated, you will spend your whole life looking for something not there, and perhaps overlook the connection that would make you feel exactly as you desire to feel.

It is rare to have a twin flame, as we have defined it, incarnated in this lifetime. Many who use this label are not referring to a twin flame as defined, but an intense connection of another type. High-level soulmate relationships and karmic soulmate relationships can have very strong similarities to twin flames in terms of relationship dynamics, but they are not technically, vibrationally the same. At the end of the day, the label does not matter. What matters is how you feel and what you know in your heart. Experiencing a twin flame connection in this incarnation is not a better or worse experience than not. It is simply a distinct one. The same as being a parent is not a better or worse experience than not, being an entrepreneur is not a better or worse experience than not, being a celebrity is not a better or worse experience than not, and so on. They are all simply different experiences, each allowing for different lessons and expansion opportunities, and all equally valuable.

And so, what makes a soul split in two? Those who experience a twin flame connection are energetically advanced souls who have a distinct mission to anchor in more light, codes of love, and new relationship templates onto the planet. That is not to say that others are not also here to anchor in light and divine love onto the planet, but twin flames carry unique divine love codes that play a prominent role in shifting the relationship experience for all on the planet. Twin flames each have their own unique missions (as do all souls here), but the shared mission of all twin flames is specifically supporting divine masculine and feminine embodiment and integration on this planet along with activating new divine love templates, which has the effect of shifting relationship paradigms overall. This has larger effects on the earth grids themselves, and the frequency of souls that are able to incarnate here next.

Twin flames are a living example of the integration of masculine and feminine energies, a physical expression of the dynamics that are playing out quite internally for many of you. By incarnating in two separate bodies, the essence can gather twice as many experiences and lessons that are necessary for growth, all in one time-space reality, and all of these data points will come together to expand the light body and energy body in a profound way when there is union between these beings, within this soul. Union refers to acceptance, integration, and energetic cohesion.

CHAPTER 36

UNION

What the twin flame journey truly represents is coming together within oneself, accepting all of oneself, and loving all of oneself. While it externally appears to be the coming together of two beings, it is the integration of one as a whole. It is a playing out of what is possible when you come into your wholeness, when you balance the energies within, and when you face all of your shadow. In a twin flame connection, there is no hiding. Twin flames will share an energy body, they will share soul memory, they will feel the energetic connection despite any physical time or space. The journey will lead them to a place where they have the opportunity to get to know themselves more deeply through learning the other. It is like watching a movie of yourself play out right in front of your eyes, being able to witness the choices you might have made in a different set of circumstances, watching your shadow play out, your fears play out, and your insecurities. Witnessing the full spectrum of you. And so, in a twin flame journey, you are completely on display. We will repeat—there is no hiding.

On the twin flame journey, you are faced with the opportunity to truly learn yourself, to integrate all of you, to love all of you, to embrace all of you, and to fully reclaim your power. Twin flame union represents full acceptance and love of oneself. It is embracing all of yourself, it is following your soul self instead of your ego, and it is choosing commitment to yourself. This is mirrored on the journey. Everything you thought you knew about relating to another will be flipped on its head because the journey is, in fact, about relating to yourself.

Meeting a twin flame will be a distinct experience for those who are self-aware and at the vibrational place to receive it. It is an intense activation that sets off a cascade of personal awakenings. This can manifest as personal or spiritual events, depending on the energetic orientation of the person. The twin who holds more of the feminine energy will experience the process differently than the twin who holds more of the masculine energy. We will remind you— the feminine and masculine energies are not related to sex or gender. A person of any sex or gender could hold more of the feminine or more of the masculine energy in the twin flame connection.

The key piece of the twin flame journey is fully activating both the divine feminine and divine masculine within each unit. And so, the divine feminine must learn to unapologetically embody the divine feminine within, transmuting any wounded or distorted divine feminine tendencies, and live from this powerful frequency by also cultivating divine masculine energy within. The divine masculine must learn to confidently embody the divine masculine within, transmuting any wounded or distorted masculine traits, and learn to love, integrate, and utilize the divine feminine within as well. It is twin flame union—the full integration of self and full acceptance of self—that turns on a powerful light grid and activation for those they are energetically connected to. It is an intense point of creation, because the union of the masculine and feminine energies—the soul choosing itself, coming together as one—is a direct mirroring of the one—of the masculine and feminine integration of Source coming together, of Source itself.

And so, united twin flames will also feel and know this responsibility deeply—living as love, activating an expansion of energetic power, anchoring in more light, knowing their mission to spread that activation to those who desire to receive it. Twin flames incarnated are feeling called to their missions. These individuals are at the end of their required incarnations. In their individual vessels, they are calibrated to a high amount of energy and have encountered a number of experiences to expand their energetic field in this incarnation, combined with the soul knowledge and wisdom they have accumulated through other incarnations and experiences. Through twin flame union, it all turns online, and they expand the limits of what they have known to be possible—energetically, emotionally, physically, and spiritually.

But there is also the very palpable experience of what it is to not embrace all of yourself, to not integrate all of yourself. Until union, it will be as though there is always one part of the generator missing. And so, this is mirrored for those who are not on the twin flame journey. When you do not embrace or love all of yourself, when you give your energy away, when you do not fully integrate all that is available to you, you are only accessing a portion of your magic, your gifts, your abilities, and your divine knowing. The difference with a twin flame experience is that this will be shown to you involving another physical person. For those without an incarnated twin flame, this will be an internal process. For all, it is by coming into energetic balance, it is by embracing and loving and seeing all of yourself, that you reclaim your gifts. It is knowing your soul so deeply and clearly. This is available to all, if you choose to accept it.

In the twin flame dynamic specifically, each aspect of the soul incarnated will have a different experience, which is part of the soul experiencing the full range of required experiences in this specific incarnation. If you were to look at the overall incarnation of each twin, you would find similarities because of the same underlying soul frequency, but you would see a balance of choices and experiences—each twin going through a different side of the coin—so the soul goes through the full range of expression and lessons in this lifetime. The full spectrum. If both twins were to express the same, make the same choices, grow up in the same circumstances, have the exact same hardships, they would still be missing a range of experiences. So there will be much crossover, particularly in terms of underlying energies, but also exact opposites in terms of life experience and personal expression.

The feminine energy will experience the lessons necessary to learn and trust her divine feminine, as well as to heal her relationship with the divine masculine—in general, and within herself— allowing the divine masculine aspect to come forward. The feminine energy will be thrust into a variety of lessons related to the soul and the spiritual realm. Many of these lessons activate while out of physical connection with the masculine. It is healing and embodying her divine feminine that energetically requires the divine masculine to activate. It is the soul work, the energetic work, that creates shifts in the material realm. And so, the divine masculine feels this, whether he is conscious of it or not. The masculine energy will experience the lessons necessary to fully embody his divine masculine, as well as to heal his relationship with the feminine—in general, and within himself—allowing the feminine aspect to come forward. The masculine energy will be thrust into a variety of lessons related to the ego and the material realm. Many of these lessons fully activate once in connection with the divine feminine. And so, while all twin flame pairs are different, it is common for the divine feminine to initially experience the connection spiritually, and for the divine masculine to become aware of the connection in some way related to the physical realm. You are meant to have slightly different experiences. It is union that brings these experiences together and activates alignment. From very different angles, you are learning the lesson of choosing soul over ego.

When it comes to union, there are four main components we will highlight. First, fully embodying both the divine masculine and divine feminine within, having transmuted any distorted or wounded versions of these traits, and living from energetic balance within oneself. Second, aligning with and living from your soul-self rather than ego. Third, aligning with your unique soul mission—the specific mission your soul came here with to activate the planet. Both twins will have involvement in this mission. Choosing it, and taking action to carry it out, whether or not the other version of you is doing the same. There is no need to wait. Fourth, true self-love—full acceptance and unconditional love for all of yourself.

CHAPTER 37

MIRRORS

The twin flame journey is about knowing oneself, choosing oneself, living in highest alignment and then watching as all aspects of your soul come into integration. For the twin flame, this is a physical person. The twin flames will feel a strong sense of mission throughout their lifetimes, although they may not know what it is. This might manifest as always searching, always feeling like something is off, always feeling as though they are missing something, always feeling like there is more. Twin flames are often prone to addictive tendencies as a way of numbing themselves because they feel energy, and responsibility, so deeply.

The experience of twin flames meeting will depend on that individual's level of self-awareness, particularly on the soul level, whether or not other activation experiences have occurred, and energetic attunement. By activation experiences, we are referring to specific experiences they are meant to go through, typically soul contract experiences, prior to being able to recognize the twin on a soul level. There are many people in your life who are here to help you learn unique lessons—your twin reflects the most for you, but there are certain lessons that others will teach you. This is why some twins don't recognize each other upon meeting, but when they come in contact at a later time, they do.

When we say energetic attunement, we are referring to—how well do they know themselves? How do they interpret their feelings? The meeting is a physical example of how one responds when they meet themselves. The twins might have different conscious responses, or they might have the same. There is an energetic activation upon meeting a twin flame that might shift the twin's life in a number of ways. This could be a change in career, relationships, living situation, desires, interests, health, spiritual gifts, or perspective. For a twin already on the spiritual path, they will notice a reactivation of dormant gifts and intensified spiritual experiences. The feminine energy will experience more of the spiritual activations after the twin flame meeting, while the masculine energy will experience more of the masculine, earthly activations. This will be more related to the material realm.

For example, the feminine might experience intuitive upgrades, kundalini rising, an expanded aura, being led to specific spiritual teachers or experiences, an emotional cascade of events, or a deepening of their connection with Source. The masculine energy might experience a shift in career, changes in family life or friendships, physical health changes, or a shifting worldview. Nothing is set in stone, but these are common themes. These changes can be experienced and perceived as positive or negative. When the same soul frequency meets itself, the energy body is supercharged, in a way. This typically leads to what you perceive as positive events. But when the soul is getting further away from itself, this typically leads to what you perceive as negative events.

Activation events and experiences are always sending you a message, aligning you with your true self.

Each twin flame pair will have been guided to specific lessons throughout their lifetime that, upon union, will be a complete set of knowledge and skills required for their unique mission, which is revealed after they choose it. Not all choose it. Not all choose themselves, their highest level of ascension, or their mission, despite your Higher Self constantly trying to guide you there. United twins are living examples of what is possible for everyone in terms of ascension—it is fully accepting, embracing, and living as your soul self. We will come back to the balance between free will and destiny—for when it is part of your path, your soul will intently push you in that direction. You can choose to stay in resistance the whole way through, or you can choose to surrender to the journey.

Imagine meeting your soul in another. Not only is this an intense energetic activation when the auras connect—turning on conscious awareness of the full energy body—but there is an inexplicable emotional activation as well. Recognizing this connection is distinct. It changes the way you perceive yourself. It transcends what you have known as love. It is beyond your experience of that, because it connects you to divine love as it is felt within yourself. It is divine love in you. It is instant knowing. It is divine recognition of self. It is your soul. To give an example, tune into the frequency of full divine love within yourself, for yourself. Tune into the frequency of love when you are connected to Source. Then, tune into full divine love as you might for a romantic partner. You will notice a slightly different undertone. The energy felt upon a twin flame activation is closer to the former two examples. The tie between twins is the tie to yourself! How that first recognition is experienced by the twin will reflect back that person's relationship with themselves, their relationship with truth, and their relationship with love from Source. One might feel fear, overwhelm, avoidance, nerves, detachment, excitement, joy, relief, or curiosity, amongst other emotions, when they meet the other incarnation of themselves. Whatever is genuinely felt is helpful information for their own inner healing.

The aligned time for the twins to meet will be when there is an energetic opening for at least one twin flame, if not both. That energetic opening will occur when one or both twins have completed all other activation events and lessons necessary prior to the initiation of the conscious part of the journey. This will set off a cascade of events where the twins are consistently given the opportunity to choose. To choose the journey, to choose themselves, to choose understanding themselves, seeing themselves, committing to themselves, and setting aside their ego. The twin flame journey will certainly hit your ego—seeing your soul expressed in another body! Seeing the ways your soul can also be expressed, witnessing someone else make decisions that energetically impact you but you perceive to not be your own, recognizing traits you wish you had more of, seeing patterns and behaviors your ego doesn't like within yourself—it is not comfortable for the ego. You are seeing all of you. Telepathy and an awareness of shared emotions will be ignited as well. The same way you are able to feel fears from other aspects of you in different incarnations or from different times, a twin flame can feel those of their twin. The twin flame experience offers an example of how your "individual" emotions, experiences, and choices in this reality, in this incarnation, are affected by and influenced by that of your soul "elsewhere." It is all connected. For the twin flames, they experience this in one reality.

And so, in twin flame communities you hear of a runner and a chaser energy, and you can perceive it as such, but running, chasing, and different steps of the journey that are often outlined are actually not requirements for the twins. The way the journey plays out is dependent on their level of self-knowledge on a soul level, how willing they are to live as their truest selves and acknowledge their truest selves, how willing they are to look at what is being mirrored for them, and how willing they are to take action in alignment with their soul. To fully embrace this journey is to learn to live your life with a boldly open heart, fully trusting your soul. What is described as running and chasing is an external show of dynamics that all, twin flames or not, experience within themselves—the times when you show up for yourself, love yourself, be your true self, and then the times when you run, you hide, you avoid admitting truths to yourself, you avoid looking certain places, and you fall into ego instead of soul.

With twin flames, it is like a play on the stage of life—a play of the internal back-and-forth many of you go through in your lifetime in the process of ascension, in the process of learning to live from your soul rather than your ego. That push and pull energy is not required, although it might be common. If you feel those aspects of you within—we will say the soul and the ego—and you feel the back and forth, understand that for twin flames this will be played out in the physical. The physical mirrors the internal state the twin is in. Where you might feel the back and forth of the divine masculine and divine feminine within you, so this is played out by the twin flames in the physical. There is a physical example of the magic that can occur when you are fully balanced within—full activation of power, alignment with soul, living as the full integration of your soul self, a direct reflection of living as Source. It is a commitment to your soul self.

The best way to know if you have met your twin flame is to know yourself deeply. When you know your soul self, you will of course recognize it within another, and meet that other with the love you also have for yourself. When one twin is in recognition and the other is not, what does this reflect back to both twins? Every imbalance in the relationship is a direct reflection of an imbalance within themselves. Where else are you not recognizing yourself? Where else are you not choosing yourself? Where are you not choosing full love for yourself? Where are you out of alignment? Where are you attached to an old version of your life? Where are you unwilling to meet new versions of yourself?

Twin flames in energetic union will create an expanded energy field that allows for the activation of more light onto the planet—more healing energy—and this will be felt by those in their field. This will, in turn, help to activate more souls around them. It also leads to a quickening in the alignment of soul family. Other souls who are resonant with them will start to activate their missions and find them if they have not already. Twin flames are often central points in friend circles—they bring people together. Twin flames incarnated for a hyper-specific mission, because they are at the end of their required time incarnating in this way to complete earth lessons. They have an opportunity to clear any energetic loose ends they might have and reach full integration. These are what you would consider very old souls, in terms of incarnation experience. Their energetic capacity is in fact so great that it cannot hold in one physical body—it is split into two. And if each individual chooses to fully activate themselves, then upon meeting and through union there is a quantum upgrade in the energetic field. It is a palpable force to even those who are energetically unaware.

It is through a twin flame journey that one is deeply humbled—to witness another version of themselves live their life. They cannot control those life choices, but can feel the energetic repercussions, the same way you might feel frustrated that energy from another incarnation, or an old experience, still affects you. One is humbled on the twin flame journey as they are able to see quite clearly where they are not showing up for themselves and where they are out of alignment with divine love. The journey is humbling because they cannot hide from their emotions. They cannot hide from their intuition. They cannot hide from the truth of their soul. It is humbling because they are pushed to surrender to being supported and to collaborate with what they perceive to be another, but really is just another aspect of themselves. And so, to stay in hyper-independence will not work. The connection is required in order to reach full soul integration and full activation of your inherent gifts.

If one twin flame is fully committed to this and does not waver in this commitment, then the only possibility is for the other twin to eventually reach that same energetic point. This is the experience of having another version of you, physically, as a guide. Allowing yourself (your twin) to be your greatest teacher, mirror, and guide. But, again, the twin flame journey mirrors the dynamics that occur within each of you "individually." Will you choose your soul self? Will you allow yourself to surrender to the journey? Will you explore, love, and embrace all of yourself? Will you recognize that your ego cannot do it all effectively?

On the twin flame journey, to reach union is to surrender to the knowing that all of you is required to fulfill your mission and to reach your highest ascension. You cannot only look certain places. You cannot leave parts of yourself in the dark or behind. You cannot get there only operating from your ego, only operating from your masculine, or only operating from your feminine. It is connection that helps you remember Source. It is connection that is the path to full integration. While the twin flame journey offers this experience in two physical vessels in one incarnation, it is the same process that is in fact playing out for each of you internally. Will you surrender to your soul self? Will you embrace and love all of yourself? Will you choose divine love for yourself? Will you integrate all aspects of you? This realigns you with your essence as divine love, as Source itself.

All of you have opportunities to meet yourself in another. It might not be your soul expressed in two different physical vessels in this exact incarnation, but from a higher perspective, remember that you are all of the One. All beings around you mirror different aspects of yourself to you, if you take the opportunity to see it. When it comes to mirroring, it might be that another individual is showing up in a way that you are also showing up. But mirroring also occurs when another person shows up in any which way, offering the opportunity for you to see how you react, how you respond, and what it brings up in you.

Mirroring doesn't have to mean you are doing the same thing as the other. It can be a reflection of any sort. What does every experience and every connection reveal to you about humanness itself? What does it reveal to you about all of the ways in which you are in alignment with your soul, and the ways in which you are out of alignment with your soul? What does it teach you about what it looks like and feels like to show up with divine love, and to not? We point this out because many of you perceive the concept of mirroring to mean what you are seeing is also what you are doing or being, but true mirroring expands out far beyond that. To understand yourself as an extension of the One is to understand that all beings around you are showcasing different expressions of that one. Observing this teaches you so much about the many aspects of oneness, whether or not all of these aspects or energies will play out or are playing out currently in your experience.

CHAPTER 38

ENERGETIC FRICTION

Soulmate connections, karmic connections, and twin flame connections are specific types of soul connections, but all relationships need not fall under labels. What is important is to simply tune into what is a vibrational match for you when you are in alignment with your soul self, in alignment with divine love. What comes forward then? Before focusing more deeply on different stages of romantic relationships, in order to further unlock these energetic dynamics we would like to speak more on the energetic friction many of you experience in relationships. Remember, all relationships are valuable, even those that did not work out as you might have expected—especially those that did not work out as you might have expected! These relationships are preparing you, teaching you, offering you the lessons required for your next higher energetic shift, helping you know yourself more and more deeply, so that you can more quickly align with your truest self. It is from this space that the most aligned divine life partner enters your reality. But the most important piece is that you fully take each opportunity to tune into yourself and learn about yourself, to integrate the lessons, and to make the energetic shifts. Otherwise, you will simply attract a different version of the same dynamic.

Fully making the energetic shift often means facing a similar situation but choosing differently. This anchors in your way of showing up differently, meeting an old energy from a higher frequency, and so the lesson is complete, the energetic shift has been made, and you will attract something different from there. But one of your biggest blocks in relationships, and where many feel trapped in the cycle of dating, of meeting different people, of getting somewhere new, is that they have not taken the time to fully explore what they were meant to learn about themselves in the last experience. They do not go into the depths of the teachings available to them. Instead, they try to simply move on. They try to forget.

Relationships—connections—are your opportunity to more deeply connect with yourself, to more deeply connect with Source, to more deeply connect with and live from your truth. Are you taking these opportunities? Or are you continuing to show up as the same version of yourself, from the same energy, with a different costume on, perhaps thinking about changes but never actually making them, and expecting to somehow attract something different? You must make the energetic shifts to see a shift in what you attract. Where are you staying in the same dynamics? Playing out the same patterns? Saying yes to what is truly a no? Not honoring your truth? This is why the energy is stuck—the vibrational shift is not made. You must first shift yourself.

If you fully squeeze the pulp out of each relationship, so to speak, in terms of personal awareness, you will find that you can make much larger vibrational shifts in less time than if you pick up simply one or two notes from each connection. It is not about how many connections you go into, or how long each connection lasts—it is about the depth of understanding yourself you squeeze out of each! This is up to you! If you want something different, show up differently. Learn from what is available to you. The connections currently in your reality, and those of your past—have you truly explored what each could teach you about yourself? This is how you make the vibrational shifts that align you with your soul's desires. Sometimes it is within the same relationship that you keep learning about yourself, and here you have a lifelong partnership. Other times, you grow the most in a relationship for a certain period of time, in certain ways, and you activate different relationships to continue learning about yourself. Some commitments will be shorter, and others will be longer—there is no right or wrong. If it is available for you to collapse the timeline in terms of attracting a romantic partner, it will be done by fully learning the lessons that have been made available to you thus far—fully exploring where you can grow, expand, and show up as the highest version of yourself. If you are blaming others in all of your relationships, then you are missing the point. Let the reflection be about you. Do not forget your own power.

Aligned relationships will have an energy of flow—of two frequencies syncing up, riding the wave together. Relationships that are not aligned vibrationally will have a texture that feels like friction underneath the dynamic—constantly butting up against each other, feeling a vibrational gap the whole way through. Listen to your intuition, your soul, your inner knowing, and the evidence of how the relationship is supporting you in uncovering and living as your highest, most aligned, most authentic self. Sometimes it is the most triggering relationships that in fact support you in living as your most authentic self. Sometimes the relationships you perceive to be the most "stable" are supporting you more in stagnation than in living your truth. It is common to get caught in the trap of familiarity, of routine, of comfortability—and this is where you lose the excitement! Sometimes it is the relationships you believe are "passionate" that are in fact a bumpy ride the whole way through, are filled with friction, and so filled with drama that there is no safe space for you to embody your most authentic self, to continue to evolve, and to live in flow. Sometimes it is the relationships you think are "boring" that are in fact most aligned—they are not filled with drama, but rather are a safe container for you to flow, to evolve, to expand. When you are used to drama, your body might misperceive safety as the opposite, because it is so unfamiliar. Recognize what you're used to, and why you are drawn to what you are drawn to.

You must tune into the resonance for yourself. When you orient from vibrational alignment with truth and love, things will become clear. Is there a vibrational gap? Are the frequencies resonant? The most aligned relationships will have vibrational resonance, and as the frequencies connect, you will feel an expansion of energies on both sides—an opening of space for both to continue to raise their frequencies and to evolve as beings. Relationships that are not fully aligned will have a vibrational gap that creates the feeling of stuckness—it is like a weight tying down your balloon. Every time you rise, you feel yourself get pulled back down again. Different wavelengths that never meet—constant friction. This is not to say there will not be challenges in an aligned relationship—these are the opportunities for growth and expansion! But facing challenges you have the opportunity to overcome together is quite different than a vibrational mismatch and energetic friction the whole way through. The relationship container should feel like flow, even if there are bumps in the stream at different points in the journey. How strong is the foundational frequency that you have built upon? This requires you to build the relationship as your most authentic self.

CHAPTER 39

CREATING YOUR RELATIONSHIPS

Are relationships hard? That is all in perception. We invite you to take care with the words you use and the assumptions you make—really, the energy behind it all. What you believe must be true of a successful relationship, you will find. Notice what your beliefs are and where you are acting, speaking, and showing up in alignment with that belief when it need not be so. You are entering an era when relationship dynamics have the opportunity to change entirely. Instead of stepping into old paradigms, old structures, and traditional ways of being, a beautiful space of non-conventionality is opening up, and this will be liberating for many of you. Instead of thinking, how do we make this work? How do we step into this box someone set up for us? You consider instead, what is the relationship container we desire to create? If this is a blank canvas, what is the art we desire to create together? What does that look like for us? What do we get to dream up together? What excites us? What nurtures us? What expands us?

Enter your relationships with the energy of co-creation. When you understand that you are a co-creator, this offers you the conscious awareness to truly co-create your own life. Why not bring that energy into the co-creation of your relationship? You look to other people to learn "how" to navigate relationships instead of creating them yourselves. What if there was no model? What if you are your own model? What if your intuition and your desires show you the model? The point is that it need not ever look the way it looked before unless you want it to. It need not look like your own previous relationships. It need not look like your partner's previous relationships. It need not look like your parents' relationship, what you have seen in the media, or what has been laid out by any institution. You get to co-create the relationship. What will you set the frequency to?

Remember, you are a creator. Many of you enter relationships forgetting you are the creator, and so you unintentionally step into an energetic template someone else set, and this is where you don't feel aligned. Every relationship is its own beautiful blank canvas, a unique mixture of frequencies, a unique piece of artwork to be created. What will your contribution be? Do you truly wish to create something you have seen before, or do you wish to expand the realm of possibility, and create that which is completely unique and authentic to who you are now? Create what you desire. The aligned match will harmonize with you, the melodies will sync, and you will flow together. But if you try to force yourself to sing someone else's tune, the music will feel discordant to both for the whole song.

We invite you to explore a new perspective. Instead of viewing relationships as hard work inherently, you might consider viewing relationships as endless opportunities for expansion. This is similar to how you could view your own personal, spiritual, soul development as hard work, or as a beautiful, exciting, challenging process. You could view climbing the mountain as hard work, or as a great adventure filled with twists, turns, and opportunities to show you all you can achieve. It is all in perspective. The "work," as you see it, is really the willingness to expand yourself. To live your truth, to be yourself, to honor your desires and needs, to communicate clearly, to take responsibility for yourself, to heal your wounds, to move beyond your conditioning, to show up with love. What if the "hard" part is just your own resistance? And so the question becomes—how committed are you to yourself? How committed are you to divine love itself? How committed are you to embodying your highest, most authentic expression? How committed are you to living your highest frequency, or what you might see as your highest potential?

On the topic of how you perceive relationships (we are discussing romantic relationships, at this point), remember the invitation to redefine relationships for yourself. What does it mean to you to be in a relationship? To be in a partnership? What is it you are truly seeking? How do you wish to feel? If you are creating it for yourself, what does that creation look like? Many of you have never even pondered the question. The key is to start to unravel what is conditioning and what is your truth. What would you like to express? What would you like to create? You need not be bound to definitions and paradigms of those who came before you, your parents, a religious institution, anything you read in a book, or anyone else's definitions or perceptions or judgments.

When it comes to the most relevant energetic blocks to allowing yourself to receive love, to committing to a relationship, to understanding your inherent worthiness and deservingness of love, in what you believe is "normal" in relationships, in how you communicate and express, and so on, most of this is conditioning, unless you have already deeply explored redefining relationships for yourself. What you learned growing up from your parents and other models around you informs what you believe to be normal or common—what you are expecting, what you are assuming, what you believe occurs in a "normal" relationship, how you think it begins, how you think it ends, what you believe it feels like, what you believe is possible, and so on. Some of the most important personal exploration work you can do is to start to unravel what you learned as a child, what was modeled to you, what stories you created from that, and how you are still living out those stories. Explore where those stories are still limiting you, where you are afraid that what happened before will happen again, what you believe is possible, what you believe are normal dynamics, and so on. What did you learn, and how did you internalize it? And then, move on to your other relationships, doing the same sort of exploration work. What did you learn, and how did you internalize it? From there, you can see where the past is projected onto the future, where you might be creating self-fulfilling prophecies that need not be created, where you are living in assumptions that are limiting you, and where you took on beliefs from other people that need not be your own.

The key is to peel apart what is serving you and what is not, and what is aligned with divine love and what is not. If you were taught that you were not allowed to have boundaries as a child, whether that be through your own relationship with a parent or watching your parent interact with others, then you might fall into people-pleasing behaviors, enabling behaviors, or feeling unsafe to stand firm in your worthiness and boundaries as an adult. What interactions led you to believe that love was something to be earned? What interactions led you to believe that you are obligated to certain people? What styles of communication were normalized? Every relationship container is different. One model is only one example of infinite possibilities.

And so, do you wish to live from what has been done before, and live out the same patterns, or do you wish to live in the realm of infinite possibility? This is where the magic lies, where the expansion lies, where you truly write your own story. What are the beliefs—the knowings—that ring true in your soul, that inspire you to fully open yourself up in relationships? What makes you feel safe, seen, heard, and loved? By unpacking these beliefs, you can explore your fears and where they come from. Are they truly yours? This is how you can rewrite the story—by shaking up what you believed was "normal" in relationships, as that is completely subjective. Just because something is common does not mean it is in your highest alignment. In fact, most of what is common is not in your highest alignment, which is why it is up to you to uphold the higher frequency and to set the example of living and being and relating from the frequency of divine love. This opens up the field for that energy to flow more easily amongst the collective.

The key to creating your reality is to shine a light on your beliefs—those that are conscious, and those beyond conscious awareness. This is your roadmap to what you are creating. From there you can reprogram the system, align your beliefs with divine love and with your highest truth, because you are the creator. Watch as your reality recalibrates. But you must be ready to look at all of yourself. Through relationships, you will see more stories come to light. You will see where old dynamics are playing out again and again. You will pause in certain moments and wonder, *when have I felt this before? What is this truly poking at within me? What belief, pattern, behavior, or area that is ready to be healed is this shining a light on?* These are the beautiful opportunities to bring more to light! The mirrors will show you your blind spots—this is the beautiful gift of connection.

CHAPTER 40

DYNAMICS IN DATING

Different relationship containers will serve different people at different times. The "answer" is always to anchor into divine love, authenticity, and truth, and allow your inner knowing to guide you to what is most resonant for you. There is not a formula, a right or wrong, or a better than or worse than, as all serves its purpose for different lessons and expansion opportunities. We will offer this—align with what you truly desire within yourself and through your connection, and then ask your soul which container supports you in that. What is it that you are truly seeking? What container will allow you to explore all of your depths, to live your truth, and to fully connect with your essence as an extension of Source? From another perspective, a valuable question is, *am I using any dynamics, behaviors, patterns, or containers as a way to avoid or hide from any part of myself?*

Again, we view relationships as a pathway to your highest connection with yourself, your fullest expression of self, your highest vibration, your highest connection with Source. Are your choices in alignment with bringing you back to your full connection with and as divine love? That is something only you can answer. We will offer, however, that many of you feel disconnected from yourselves because you are disconnected from your relationship with and as Source. You do not take the time to slow down and get to know yourself. That is reflected in your relationships. The depth of the connection in any relationship will be a reflection of how well you truly know yourself on a soul level. The feeling of connection, of fulfillment, of purpose, of flow that so many of you seek comes from deeply knowing yourself, remembering your direct connection to Source itself, and remembering your essence as divine love, as an extension of Source itself.

After taking time to go inward and anchor into truth and love, the next level is to allow any blind spots to be mirrored through connection. A committed partnership that is aligned with the frequency of divine love allows you to see and know more of yourself, and allows you deeper connection with the divine, with Source itself. When you are running around, staying busy, avoiding depth of any sort, avoiding being fully seen, do not be surprised if you feel disconnected and out of alignment. Remember, focus adds energetic momentum. Where is your energy divided? When you focus your energy in a clear direction, the energy moves, it flows, it expands, it penetrates, it deepens, it opens up more of what is fully available. Where you are divided, where you are in avoidance, where you are keeping busy energetically, where you are hiding, where you are distracted—this is where you are not accessing all of yourself. This is where you are disconnected from yourself. This is where you are disconnected from Source, and from divine love. What is it you wish to create in your life? Are your actions aligned with that?

This brings us to the topic of dating—specifically, attracting in your aligned partner. We have already touched on important aspects of the dating process—knowing yourself first, aligning with the truest version of yourself, holding your frequency, being aware of what feels resonant for you rather than taking on the projections or feelings of others, and re-perceiving the purpose of dating as exploring connections with different frequencies, thus bringing more of yourself to light. We will add a few more points here. The way much of your dating world has evolved has become rooted in the vibration of inauthenticity, fear, and scarcity. You have an opportunity to transmute that. You need not take part in that unless you desire to. But for an authentic connection to grow, you must be anchored into your own most authentic self. Notice what methods of dating, patterns, behaviors, actions, and ways you're showing up are because they are authentic to you and because your soul has guided you there, and which are simply unconscious programs playing out because of what has been normalized—programs coming from scarcity, lack, or illusions.

If you were truly anchored into the knowing that when you release what is not truly a vibrational match for you, it creates space for what is aligned, would you show up differently? If you knew you could attract the most aligned, authentic match, would you show up differently? Many of you engage in dating dynamics with an energy of scarcity, believing it is difficult to find someone. Notice how often you affirm that to yourself. It will be so if you believe this. Many of you engage in dating dynamics from an inauthentic place—putting on masks, adjusting yourself to the other person, because you believe this will make you more likable. Well, it might, to someone who is not truly resonant for you, and then you will see how that plays out. It is exhausting to be inauthentic.

Be anchored in the foundational frequency from which you wish to build—authenticity and love. If someone is not resonant, then you can send gratitude for the experience and learning lessons, knowing that each brings you closer to your most aligned match. Each experience is important! There is so much to appreciate in each. The universe will send you different opportunities, and you can say yes or no, refining the vibrational request until you attract what is most aligned on a soul level. The nuance here is to tune into where you are telling yourself you desire something, when it is really the want of the ego. It is still attachment to the outcome, to the who or where or when, to what the person looks like, to what they do, to where they come from, and so on. Release your attachment and anchor in the frequency that is most resonant with your soul.

Allow your soul to guide you. Allow your soul to surprise you with how your desires are delivered. Can you allow yourself to be pleasantly surprised? Notice where you are playing the games—this is where you are not strong in your energetic resilience. Notice where you are continuing to say yes to people who are not showing up for you, who are not reciprocating, and who are making excuses. When you do, you are telling the universe that, in fact, this is what you want more of. When you continue to engage in the experience, the energetic message sent is that this is a "yes" for you. Notice where you are complaining about attracting more of what you are saying yes to, by continuing to engage with it! We are pointing this out with love because many of you feel that dating is so much more difficult than it really is, and we invite you to view it from a more neutral perspective.

Are you fully showing up as the vibrational match for what you want? Are you showing up as the version of yourself you desire to be, in terms of how you feel and express yourself, from the beginning? Are you showing the clearest, truest version of you? Are you upholding your energetic requirements and your most authentic frequency? Or are you chasing after someone who is not meeting you? Are you enabling the games? Are you engaging with someone who does not honor you? This first starts with honoring yourself. Here we come back to the important tasks before productively engaging in any period of dating—knowing, honoring, and loving yourself. When you know, honor, and love yourself—because you recognize your inner beauty, your essence as love, how incredible you truly are, and your own divinity—you treat yourself from that space of honor. It is from this vibration that you also see the divinity and love in others. It is from this vibration that you also honor others, treat them with respect, and show up with integrity.

When someone is not showing up with respect and integrity, this is in fact a reflection of their relationship with themselves. When you observe the common patterns and styles of energy exchange in dating contexts, are they aligned with honor and respect for each other? If they are not, and you recognize this, you can redirect your energy. Show up from the energy you desire, and you will attract more of that to you. There are many conscious individuals who are ready for an aligned, truly loving connection. Will you allow yourself to receive that? That means letting go of whatever you're trying to force to work. You must be honest about where you are in attachment, where you are in a scarcity mindset, where you are in the belief it's not possible or it's difficult, and where you are in the belief that you are not worthy of divine love. In what ways are you self-sabotaging? In what ways are you settling? This is where you are not honoring your divinity! This is where you are forgetting your truth, and your power as co-creator in your own life! This is where you are forgetting your own magnetism.

Remember, everything you engage with is an energetic signal. Reflect on the question, *why am I giving my time, energy, and attention to a dynamic, person, or situation that does not honor and respect me?* Reflect on the question, *am I showing up in a way that is aligned with divine love? Am I showing up in a way that is in alignment with respect, love, and integrity for another? And for myself?* It is from the frequencies of respect, love, and integrity that the aligned action flows.

CHAPTER 41

SOUL-LED AND EGO-LED ATTRACTION

You must first be clear in what you desire from soul, not ego. There is a difference between soul-led attraction and ego-led attraction. Soul-led attraction will align you with a relationship that is truly vibrationally resonant and has space for you to expand and evolve, while ego-led attraction will align you with what makes sense, what feels safe, and what is limited in its vibrational depth. It is when you follow your ego over your soul that you unknowingly limit yourself. And so, how is it you desire to feel? Safe, loved, limitless, connected, expanded, supported, seen, heard, loved, respected? What are you looking for in a connection? Are you looking for someone who meets you where you are at, or someone who will grow and expand with you? What are the energies that are aligned with the most expanded version of you? Are you open to the ways in which this might be delivered?

When you are clear on what you desire, you must first ask if you are a vibrational match for that. How are you showing up? Do you embody the energies you are looking for in a relationship? If not, then this is where you are using the relationship to fill your holes. This is where you are putting expectations on another that are truly just a reflection of where you are not showing up as the fullest version of yourself. Anchor into your why. What is the foundational frequency of the want? If it is from shame that you are not already in a relationship, if it is from scarcity, if it is from not feeling whole yourself, if it is from avoiding responsibility, or if it is from looking for someone else to make you happy, then you are building on a cracked foundation, and that frequency will be threaded throughout the connection. Build from the foundational frequency you wish to carry through the relationship—wholeness, honesty, love, authenticity, enjoyment.

You must first show up as the version of yourself you want to be in the relationship, and the version of yourself that is a match for what you wish to attract, in order for it to come into your reality. Notice where you are waiting for a relationship to develop in order for you to feel a certain way or do a certain thing. This relates to creating energetic space. Many of you unintentionally put up blocks to receiving an aligned match because there is no space—you are too busy working, you are always with friends, you are carrying too many worries or burdens, you are always on the move. Is there emotional space for that person? Are you ready to hold space? Are you ready to be seen? Is there physical space? Is there room in your life, in your schedule, in your place of living? Is there energetic space? If you are comfortable in your life and not willing to make space, then do not be surprised if the person does not arrive.

Many of you do not receive the relationships you desire because you do not want to "give up" certain things. You do not want to give up old patterns, habits, space, time, or relationships. Notice what underlying stories you are living from. What is it you fear, deep down, you will miss out on, lose, or have to give up when you are in a relationship? This is where you are unintentionally blocking it from coming in. For example, if you have built a belief that your career will suffer when you are in a relationship, and focusing on your career is a top priority for you, do not be surprised if you find energetic blocks with meeting your divine life partner. If you have built a belief that your friendships will change, that the way you take care of yourself will have to change, that you won't be able to travel as much, or that you'll have to take on responsibilities you don't really want to take on, then don't be surprised if you are unintentionally blocking yourself from receiving the manifestation!

Your subconscious beliefs are what you must consider when looking at attraction. What stories have you created? You say you desire something, but do you really? Is there a piece of you that doesn't truly desire it? Is there a piece of you that is already anticipating rejection? Abandonment? Burden? Drama? Sacrifice? Having to give up things that are important to you? This is where you will block yourself from attracting in your most aligned match. First bring these stories to light, and then rewrite them. For example, if the energetic block to calling in your most aligned partner is that you are expecting to have to spend less time with your friends, which you do not want to do, then simply shift that belief, and call in a partner where you feel perfectly balanced with friendships and romantic relationships.

The truth is that much of what you believe you have to "give up," you do not truly have to in an aligned partnership. Anywhere that the energy is recalibrated will not feel like giving anything up because you will be in the divine flow of love. Many people say they do not want to "give up" unhealthy foods, but when they start nourishing their bodies with nutrient-dense foods, they feel so amazing that they don't perceive it to have been giving anything up at all. If anything, what they gave up was feeling unwell. And so, where is your ego blocking you from aligning fully with your desires?

If you are afraid of change, then don't expect to attract anything different than where you are at right now. A change in your reality will require a change in you. And a change in the type of relationship dynamic you have will also require a change in you. You must show up fully with love, fully in your truth, fully in your authenticity—being clear with your frequency. Where are you settling for the best you think you can get? Where are you telling yourself you are not worthy of divine love, or that you are not worthy of respect? This first begins with loving and respecting yourself, releasing any illusions, judgment, or projections from others, and recognizing that you are inherently worthy of that which you are—love! If you are showing up with and as divine love, then it is not "too much" to call forward someone who reciprocates.

Where you are settling is where you are sending an updated energetic signal to the universe, as your choices are telling the universe what is a vibrational yes for you and what is a no for you. Be clear in your intention. What we wish to distinguish, however, is the difference between settling on a soul level and settling on the level of the ego. It is the ego's fear of settling that keeps many in the pattern of non-commitment, believing the grass is always greener. This often unintentionally manifests as showing up in ways that do not honor the other from a place of divine love, and this is not what we are referring to. The fear of settling, from the ego, is a common way in which many self-sabotage. This energy is a subtle reason why some never let anyone get close enough to really see them. They try to protect themselves by never putting themselves in a position to be rejected, abandoned, or deeply seen. However, through the same choices, they never receive what they truly crave—divine love, divine connection. This is not the ideal energetic space to be dating from, as we see it. In this space, one's energy is best spent understanding, knowing, and loving yourself, and getting clear on what you truly desire.

If you are dating and engaging with others, we invite you to do so from an energy of love rather than an energy of fear. Showing up with love also means clear communication about your desires and intentions with others. Some might be dating for long-term partnership, while others might be dating simply for the sake of connecting with different souls. All of this serves its purpose, but to align with love is to be clear in your communication and intentions, so everyone is on the same page. This is honoring others. Honoring others follows from honoring and respecting yourself.

Notice where you are attracted to someone on a soul-level, and notice where you are attracted from the level of the ego. This will correlate to the dynamic of the relationship. It will relate to its depth, the opportunities for expansion, and the creative capacity in all forms. Many of you are used to relating over common struggles, complaining, gossip, and surface-level hobbies and activities. Your soul is craving more. Your soul is craving to be deeply seen, loved, and heard. Your soul is craving to bond through joy, play, love, creation, honesty, vulnerability, dreams, goals, curiosities, excitements, inspiration, and celebration! To shift into relating from divine love will dissolve the bonds over struggle, complaining, gossip, and low-frequency conversation. The conversation will shift, and the resonance will shift.

You might find that in connections based on ego-level or mental-level attraction, you suddenly don't have much to say, because you are ready to connect through higher frequencies, and anything else leaves you feeling low and unsatisfied. From here we will explain that loving from the matrix is different from loving from the soul. What has been normalized in your society is loving from the matrix, which we do not see as aligned with the divine definition of love, but rather an infatuation, addiction, or interest based on conditioning and illusions. This is aligned with underlying expectations, religious and societal programming, and what you have been shown in mainstream media—aligning with someone based on what makes sense to the ego or the mind. This is different from loving from the soul, which is based on vibration, which is based on soul resonance, which is aligned with the divine definition of love.

As the frequency of the planet shifts, many will find relationships that served them at their old frequency will no longer fulfill them as they are activated to living as their highest selves. In other words, what worked before will not anymore. Dating advice that worked before will not anymore, particularly because most dating advice has been based on feeding into the illusions and the games. Many have approached dating from an energy of, *how do I adjust myself or someone's perception of me so that they find me attractive?* If anything sets you up with an unstable foundation, it is this. Honesty is the way forward. You must be honest with yourself, and from there you can be fully honest with others. But what fulfilled you before, at another frequency, will no longer fulfill you, because it is depth and it is soul resonance you desire.

As you are activated to higher frequencies and step into sovereignty, you will not outsource your needs and desires as you did before, and what you are looking for in terms of relationship will shift as well. Partnership has had many uses in your society, and in fact, much of them were based on safety, stability, comfort, and companionship in the 3D sense. As you find this within yourself, you will be craving something else. You will be looking for connections that support your expansion and that bring you closer to Source. If it is neutral, it will not be serving you—it will take up energetic space. We are explaining this now so you can be conscious of what you are currently aligning with and how you are showing up. Where you are playing into old paradigms is where you might find yourself frustrated and unfulfilled. Anchor into authenticity, soul resonance, soul-led vibrational attraction, and you will receive what is truly a soul-level match. Feed into stories, illusions, and inauthenticity, and do not be surprised when you feel vibrationally capped. Loving from the soul is loving from your divinity. It is the most healing, powerful frequency. It is that which you have always been seeking, because it is your truth. And the more you live as that vibration, the more you attract it to you.

As you show up as the most authentic version of yourself, as you choose to feel the way you want to feel right now, and as you create energetic space for what you are calling in, you surrender to the process. You allow it to be delivered in the right timing, in whatever way is for your highest and best. Notice whether you are attached to the when or the how—this is how you push it away. If you were truly ready vibrationally, it would have already come! All you must do is open your eyes to what is coming forward in your reality—these are the clues as to what is meant to be looked at, healed, cleared, and upgraded for you to become a vibrational match. Perhaps it is another relationship to be released, a self-sabotaging pattern, an area where you do not feel you are enough, perhaps it is a different career choice, perhaps it is learning to love dating yourself, or perhaps there are other lessons that must come through in different relationships first. Have you fully embraced these opportunities and made the energetic shifts from each lesson? From here you watch it be delivered as it is meant to, in perfect timing. If you have decided what the "right" and "wrong" time is from your ego, if you want it to come through on a certain timeline or in a certain way from your ego, this is where you do not trust yourself. When you fully trust yourself and your power as a co-creator, you are not concerned about the timing. That concern is a worry it will not come in at all, but if you know your magnetism and power as a co-creator, you need not worry about this. Notice how the worry itself becomes what you are focusing on, and then what you are energizing in your reality. Stay in the frequency you desire to feel. Hold the frequency. Hold the knowing. It is being delivered in perfect timing.

CHAPTER 42

RESONANT FREQUENCIES

You might also wonder, when it comes to dating, how is it that two people can feel so differently about each other? Many have experienced an interest in another but not felt that reciprocated, and we will offer to you that this is a gift of simply knowing what is a match and what is not. You can create stories in your mind about why it wasn't a match and what it means about you, but most of this is an illusion. Most of this is your ego, your mind, and your insecurities, looking for a reason why it didn't work, what you did wrong, what that person did wrong, and so on. What if no one has to be wrong? What if no one has to be better than or worse than, good enough or not? Rather than personalizing so much of it, we simply see it as a redirection for you to more quickly attract in your aligned match. A timesaver, if you will.

Not everyone will be resonant, and that does not make anyone wrong or right, better or worse.

What is attractive is individual to each being. It is not objective. It is simply vibrational. Some of you will love the scent of lavender, while others will not. This does not mean anything about lavender itself. Some of you will love jazz music, while others will not. This does not mean anything about jazz music itself. It is simply a reflection of how certain frequencies resonate with each other and some do not, and this is a built-in filtering system for you to find what is your aligned match! Sometimes resonance changes over time, and sometimes it doesn't. Where the frequencies do not align might be due to nonresonance on a soul frequency level, but it might also be due to a mismatch in energetic availability, or it might be due to misaligned timing. These are all different sorts of nonresonance. Perhaps that person is simply not an aligned match on a soul level. Perhaps one of you is not energetically ready to receive love. Perhaps the frequency is too palpable—this might occur when you genuinely feel a resonance, but that person seems to run away, out of the blue. The meeting of frequencies might have triggered something in them, and they might not be ready to see it, or they might be afraid to receive it, or they might not be as prepared as they thought they were. Either way, there is no need to direct your energy toward what is not ready for you. If it is not aligned right now, then it is not aligned right now. And perhaps that meeting was exactly what it was supposed to be—a catalyst. Direct your energy toward what is ready for you, and what is aligned.

Be careful not to get so lost in potentials that you are distracted from what is currently available for you, and what you deserve. Remember, you do not need to convince what is for you to also desire you. What you desire on a soul level is also desiring you—it is simply about aligning with it. To do that, you must be open to how it gets delivered.

It might not be from the person your ego wants it to be. Notice where you are spending your time trying to convince someone to be aligned with you, and to desire you. This is pointing to where you are still operating from a wound, where you are still looking for external validation, where there is a piece of you that still needs to be loved and cared for more deeply by you—no one else. Divine love does not require convincing.

Another aspect to consider is that part of the dating process is uncovering what aligns and what doesn't, what feels good and what doesn't. You discover this through being in the process, not just thinking about it. You discover this through how you feel as you move through it—when you go through experiences that perhaps you thought would feel resonant and then, through the energetic exchange, you realize they do not, and so you recalibrate from there. Part of this is honoring everyone's learning and growth process, and this brings us back to viewing dating as different opportunities to learn and connect with different frequencies, to learn about yourself more and more each time. When the feelings are not reciprocated, this is also a beautiful space to reflect on what it was that drew you to that person initially. Was it mental attraction? Attraction led from the ego? Was it soul-led attraction? Was it attraction based on familiarity? This is where you can see where you were led by your soul or your ego. This is where you can see what expectations or assumptions you are still living out of. Through this exploration, you can confirm whether something you desired is in fact resonant and supports your highest frequency or if it does not.

What about when someone's feelings change seemingly overnight? Well, this is where you must swallow the truth that emotions do shift. Many of you look for security by looking for something never-changing. This is choosing stagnation. Feelings can change. Frequencies can shift. Committing to a relationship is not based on feelings never changing—it is committing to the entire process of what it is meant to be. What we will say is this—sometimes feelings change overnight because a vibration has been recalibrated, an energetic shift has been made, or a realization has occurred. Sometimes feelings shift overnight because one has realized that what they were telling themselves with their minds does not align with their hearts, and they have finally reached a point of honesty with themselves. Sometimes feelings shift because one has bumped up against a fear or pattern of self-sabotage, and so they shut down out of fear of rejection or abandonment. Sometimes feelings shift overnight because the contract is complete, and a new contract is meant to begin. Your feelings guide you to these new contracts. Sometimes feelings seem to shift overnight simply because one was not fully honest with themselves or the other person, intentionally or unintentionally.

In matters of love, many confuse their own feelings with those of the other person. Many feel the emotions of the other, and take them on as their own. In matters of love, many fall into the trap of not listening to their intuition, that nudge inside, because they are attached to an outcome, because they want to make it work, because it makes sense to the logical mind, because that person is perfect on paper—or so they think! But are they an ideal match for you? Are they of true soul resonance, which is the key factor for depth in connection? Remember, your soul can see what your mind and ego cannot, and your soul speaks to you through your intuition. It does not always make sense. Feelings do not always make sense. But they do indicate truths inside you that need to be looked at.

When there are unreciprocated feelings, this is an opportunity to explore how you might have attached to a story, a projection, a hope, or a potential, rather than the truth of what is. These are opportunities to more deeply discern the voice of your soul, the tone of your intuition. Sometimes unreciprocated feelings are something that you unintentionally attracted into your field. If you do not feel worthy of love, if you do not believe someone can love you the way you wish to be loved, if you are afraid to be seen, if you are expecting rejection, if you are expecting abandonment, then these energies have momentum in your field, and situations will come into your reality that mirror these frequencies until you shift the story. These are the self-fulfilling prophecies that keep many of you stuck in beliefs. The way out is shifting the story, shifting the energy, and acting and choosing in alignment with that energetic shift. You must show up differently!

When you shift your expectations, when you are anchored in your inherent worth and value, when you expect to receive that which you give, when you are truly ready to be loved, then watch what comes into your field. And sometimes, unreciprocated feelings are exactly what is meant for you to remember your inherent worthiness, to see how much you have grown, to notice how much you have expanded when you respond by simply sending gratitude for the experience and moving forward, rather than creating stories about what it means about you or the other person. It is through your reaction to these experiences you can notice what you truly believe about yourself, love, and relationships. And so, what a gift for these illusions to be brought to light, so you can shift the illusions to divine truth.

And what of jealousy? Jealousy is a low-frequency emotion that is indicating valuable information to you, as all emotions do, about a place in yourself where you do not feel whole, worthy, or deserving, a place in yourself where you are not fully aligned with love, where you might still be living in scarcity, lack, or fear. Before labeling something jealousy, tune into if that is truly what you are feeling, or if what you are feeling is actually inspiration or excitement about a possibility of something you could have. If you are looking at another's relationship, for example, and feeling "jealousy," is it truly jealousy, or is it a desire to feel that which is expressed in the other relationship? If so, you are able to celebrate that relationship, and in doing so, tell the universe you would like to call that energy into your own life. If it is available to someone else, it is available to you! The world is your menu! When you attach high-frequency emotions to things you desire, such as expressing gratitude for and celebrating something you see in your reality that you also desire, you send out an energetic signal that you are also desiring that thing, and that you are a vibrational match for that thing.

But what of true jealousy? This is where you believe that what another has is not available to you, and this is where you are still living in the illusion of lack. What of jealousy in partnership? When you are jealous of an interaction? When you are jealous of someone you care about being in another relationship? We invite you, as always, to use that jealousy to tune deeper into yourself. What is that interaction pointing to and triggering within you? If you are in a relationship and jealous of your partner's interactions with others, this is pointing perhaps to where you need to communicate more clearly about how you wish to be loved, and how things make you feel. It might also be pointing to where you are not anchored into your own worthiness and deservingness. It might also be pointing to where you do not trust—your partner or yourself. If you fear that your partner is going to leave you for someone else, where does that fear come from? Has their behavior suggested that? If so, is the partnership truly aligned with divine love? If their behavior has not suggested that, then what story are you living from? What are you projecting onto them? Where are you still not feeling whole within yourself? And our first question would be—how much of your own feelings have you communicated with your partner directly, instead of creating stories in your mind?

If someone is going to reject or abandon you, then worrying about it certainly will not stop that behavior. In fact, it would save you time and energy for that behavior to come to light rather than wait around wondering if it will. We suggest clear, upfront communication. And if someone betrays you in a committed partnership, that is a reflection of them, not of your worthiness. Their actions are a reflection of a deeper truth—where they are still in fear, where they are judging themselves, where they are not communicating clearly, where they are still operating from ego, where they do not know themselves, where they are afraid of true love, where they are expecting rejection, where they do not honor themselves or others, or where they are not aligning with their highest selves. It will be different in every situation. But if the feeling of jealousy is stemming from suspicions due to someone's energy, actions, or behaviors, that is an important place for you to look in terms of evaluating if it truly is an aligned partnership. Again, begin with clear communication, as sometimes you create suspicions due to wounds from past experiences. But assuming there is crystal clear communication and you are not perceiving or assuming from your wounds, remember that relationships aligned with the frequency of divine love will not leave you questioning integrity, honor, or respect. Where fears, worries, and jealousy pop up are either a reflection of fears, insecurities, and wounds that still need more love within yourself, or a reflection of your intuition indicating what is not a vibrational match. The truth always rises.

If you are worrying about it, then where does this point to where you fear truth itself? To feel jealousy in itself indicates something important to learn about yourself, for it is pointing to places where you are still not feeling good enough. No matter how it plays out, this is a crucial moment of mirroring for you. If you were fully confident in your wholeness, if you were not outsourcing your love, and if you truly loved all of yourself, jealousy and attachment would not come into play. Because you would trust that what is for you will stay in your reality. You would know that what is for your highest and best comes to you. You would trust that any dynamics that shift are for your highest and best. You would know that you have the ability to attract your soul's desires simply by being yourself. We understand this might touch a tender place for many of you, but these moments of self-reflection are the way to liberation from illusions, to living as divine love, to sourcing the love you desire from within yourself, to knowing that you can always maintain your highest vibration no matter what anyone else's actions or choices are. Another person's actions or choices are not a reflection of you—they are a reflection of them. You always choose how you respond and how you interpret, as does every other.

CHAPTER 43

CLEAR COMMUNICATION

This naturally leads us into our discussion of communication, which is one of the most important pieces of learning to relate with and from divine love. This is where the energetic resilience lowers for many of you. You are firm in your inner knowing and your vibration when alone, but why is it that something shifts when you are relating to another? Most of you are not taught to communicate clearly. But communication, as you know, is the key to co-creation. It is clearly communicating what you desire to the universe that allows you to direct the energy so it flows to you, and this is how you co-create your reality. It is clearly communicating in relationships that allows you to co-create the relationships you desire. Without crystal clear communication, how is it known what you desire? Communication comes in many forms—energetic, verbal, physical, emotional. When you know yourself deeply, you will also know your desires, your love language, your energetic requirements, and what you need to live as the fullest, highest expression of yourself. Only from that clear knowing within yourself can it be communicated to others. Where are you expecting others to know what you desire and need without communicating it?

Remember, every relationship dynamic is unique. In relationships, you bring together different "norms." Clear communication allows for the most aligned, authentic co-creation of the unique relationship dynamic. For example, what has been normalized in terms of communication styles will be different for different people, and will be different in different relationships. If you are expecting to communicate in a certain way, with a certain frequency, based on what you have done before, this might be different than what the other person has experienced in their relationships, and so you are both bringing different expectations to the relationship. When these are unspoken, this is when you feel let down, this is when you create stories, this is when you tell yourself they are not showing up for you, that they do not love you, and so on.

Be crystal clear in communicating your expectations and desires, and be open to something even better dropping in! What if, through communicating, your partner brings forward a style of relating that you have not encountered before? And what if it feels even more aligned for you than what you have experienced before? If you are coming together with another artist to create a painting, do you sit in silence and both start to paint? Or do you communicate about the vision, the feeling, and how you will collaborate? And so it is the same with co-creating a divine partnership. If you want your co-created relationship to feel different than it has before, if you want it to feel even better than you could have imagined, it will require new dynamics and a different way of showing up. This is where you can get creative!

Communicate how you want to be loved, and be open to new experiences. What feels good for you? How do you give and receive love, and how does your partner? When you honor and love another, is it not the greatest gift for them to share with you the exact code for them to feel loved? Lay it all out on the table. You already know how operating from subconscious beliefs affects you personally in your own life, and you know the value of bringing it all to the surface so you can evaluate what is serving you and what is not. It is the same in relationships, even more so when there is more than one set of underlying beliefs, conditioning, fears, expectations, assumptions, and previous experiences at play. What are the rules of engagement, so to speak? What are your energetic requirements? Your personal needs? What are your nonnegotiables? What have you learned about yourself? How are you showing up for each other? How will you address conflict or disagreements in a healthy way? What does commitment mean to you? What supports you in feeling loved, and what does not? What will it look like to grow together? How are you planning to consistently nourish and explore the relationship, yourselves, and each other? What is it that allows you to feel clear, balanced, and aligned? What lowers your vibration? What are your priorities? What is your communication style? What are you currently exploring within yourself? What have you yet to explore? What do you want to explore? How are you currently growing? How can your partner support you in this? What might they need to know about previous experiences you've had, previous stories you have told yourself, expectations, assumptions, or insecurities? It is better to bring it all to the surface so it is clear what is yours and what is not. You need not project your past onto your future.

Clear communication is required for collaboration. In a truly aligned, resonant, authentic partnership, you will feel safe to communicate clearly and with love. You will notice that in soul-resonant divine partnerships, the communication shifts. There is no more walking on eggshells. There is no judging, blaming, or projecting. There is sharing and receiving with an open heart. There is exploring. There is taking responsibility and accountability. There is support. There is excitement for what lights each of you up. There is a desire to co-create. There is a shift into solution-oriented exploration rather than problem-finding thinking. There is an energy of genuine curiosity. It is expansive, not limiting. It is loving, honoring, and respectful. It is a safe space to grow, to explore, and to expand. It is a soft space to land. It is also a container that holds the vibration, that holds you accountable with love, that challenges any beliefs or fears that might be limiting you, that shines a light on illusions and inauthenticity, that lovingly pushes you to be the clearest, brightest, most authentic version of yourself.

This is only possible with clear communication. In what ways are you afraid to communicate how you truly feel? Communicating how you truly feel and what you truly need will anchor a relationship that is truly aligned. If clear communication pushes someone away, then this is a clear sign that the relationship is not a vibrational match. When you show up at the frequency of love and respect with clear communication and someone runs away, it is because they are not a match for clear communication. This is indicating their fear of direct truth. This is helpful to realize early on! Notice where you beat around the bush, where you are afraid of saying or being too much, and where you tell yourself you are a burden. These are all stories!

How would you communicate if you knew you were unconditionally loved? This is available in a divine partnership, and it is such a healing space—a space where you can allow yourself to communicate clearly, and witness how it is received with love! In order for someone to truly, deeply see you and know you, you must allow them to. Clear communication is how you open that door. Clear communication is how you allow yourself to receive love. If you are frustrated with another's communication, the question becomes—is there anywhere you are not clearly communicating? Is there anywhere you could communicate more effectively or clearly? This is about knowing yourself and being confident in your truth.

There is often a connection between unclear communication and fear of being seen, fear of judgment, and feeling unworthy. When you are living as divine love, when you fully authentically love yourself, you do not wish to hide! You wish to be clear—to share your frequency clearly, with potency and with love. The only way for others to see you is if you communicate who you are. Remember, communication comes in many forms. It is verbal. It is physical. It is emotional. It is energetic. It is authentic confidence that leads to the clearest communication. When you are afraid to be clear with communication, this is an opportunity to find the places where your confidence can be nurtured, as these are the places you have forgotten your inherent worthiness and beauty as an extension of Source itself.

If you struggle with communication, we invite you to explore how you communicate with yourself, as well as your relationship with truth. Do you know yourself? Do you explore yourself? Have you gotten to know yourself? Do you speak your truth to yourself? Or do you sugarcoat your feelings? Do you tell yourself things are fine when you feel differently? Do you stay so busy you never have time to communicate with yourself, to communicate with the divine, or to communicate with Source? This is where the clarity comes from. Know yourself. Get comfortable with the truth within yourself. This opens up the energy for you to be able to express clearly to others. If you do not know what needs to be expressed, you will have a difficult time expressing it. Clear communication is a divine gift of love. Do you not receive it as such?

If you fear receiving clear communication, why is that? If you fear clear communication, do not be surprised when others are not clear with you! Love is truth. Truth is love. To communicate your truth is a gift of love—it is a sharing of your heart, an opening of your energy field, an invitation in. When the relationship is anchored in divine love, it is a beautiful gift to exchange. It is the way to deeper connection, to deeper love, to deeper exploration—that which you truly seek from a relationship. It is the only way to actively co-create a relationship of divine love, because energy is always shifting. Without clear, updated communication, things will get lost in translation. Dynamics are always shifting. Each of you is always shifting, changing, and growing. New seasons of life begin, and you will uncover new things about yourself, and so new rules of engagement will need to be discussed. The vision must stay updated. You get to consistently learn your partner again and again and again! Without clear communication, a vibrational gap can be unintentionally created. To choose a relationship is not just choosing one partner—it is choosing every version of their most authentic self. It is choosing to explore their multidimensionality. It is clear communication that opens the door to this endless discovery, to this endless exploration, to this endless depth, to the endless new experiences and dynamics that are available between you. Divine love is certainly never boring!

Most of your conflict, misunderstandings, and breakdowns in relationships are because of unclear communication. You will find that you can shorten timelines and attract in aligned partners much more quickly when you release expectations and practice clear communication. Many of you know when things are off, when your needs are not being met, and when you are not feeling how you desire to feel far before you ever communicate it. The sooner you communicate, the sooner the energy can shift. The sooner the truth rises, the better you will feel. Notice where you do not open the door for clear communication because you are afraid to see the truth. Holding in truths and feelings only weighs you down vibrationally. They are heavy on your system.

When those feelings are rooted in sadness, anger, resentment, guilt, shame, or unworthiness and are not expressed in one way or another, they are stored in the system. This keeps your frequency lower and leads to dis-ease in the system. More of that energy can build in the system. Instead of allowing that energy to get stuck, to fester, or to build, express it! Move it out and through. You will find that the more you practice clear communication, the more the energy in your relationship flows, the less conflicts and misunderstandings you have, and the sooner you can focus on more exciting things in your relationship rather than always focusing on recovery and repair. You will also be able to recognize sooner rather than later when a relationship is no longer aligned. When it is not aligned for one of you, it is not aligned for both of you. But you will also notice that it is clear communication that offers the space for you to be pleasantly surprised. It is through clear communication that you will notice where you had subconscious expectations of not being received well, of not being met with divine love, of what happened before happening again. What a beautiful opportunity to be proven wrong! When the relationship is aligned with divine love, there is no need to fear clear communication. Rather, it is a beautiful gift, a loving energy exchange between hearts.

CHAPTER 44

WHEN THE CONTRACT IS UP

What do you do when you are in a relationship and things do not feel in alignment? When you are no longer on the same wavelength? This is where, we will remind you, you must anchor into full love and honesty for yourself, knowing that what is in highest alignment for you on a soul level is also in highest alignment for all others involved. Many of you keep yourselves stuck in situations that are not for your highest and best because of what you think about someone else. You say you stay for someone else, because of someone else, or that you are worried how it will affect someone else. The way we see it, this is one way of putting blame on someone else for your unwillingness to live in your truth. We understand that living your truth requires bravery, but you have this within. It is not always comfortable for the ego to live your truth. Remember—you are courageous! You are love! Live from this frequency.

If you wish to create a life that is anchored in love and truth, your choices must come from this. When you are choosing something that is out of alignment with your truth, you will feel the nonresonance. This is where you are keeping your frequency lower, you feel the heaviness, you feel the stuckness, and you dull your magnetism and your abilities. Choose from love—this is also from the greatest love for yourself. To truly love another is to support them in receiving what is also for their highest and best on a soul level and is to allow them to receive exactly what they desire on a soul level, which might be different than what their ego wants. If they desire a reciprocated, loving relationship, and you are not feeling that energetic match, it is not acting from true love to stay in the relationship. Would you desire to be in a relationship if you knew the other person felt they were settling in some way, felt there was nonresonance, or was not completely in? Someone who gives a resounding, 100% yes to being in a relationship with you is available to you. It is available for all. But where you stay in anything less is where you also block that opportunity for both yourself and another. It is of highest love to create space for that other when you know it is not a vibrational match.

Before making that decision, we will remind you to first anchor into your most authentic self. Live from truth and love for yourself, and in the relationship, if you are to clearly see what is working and what is not. If you are unhappy in the relationship, this is not because of the other person. Your happiness is sourced from yourself. There might be dynamics that are not resonant for you—but that is the co-creation of both of you, not just the other person. There might be dynamics that are not healthy for you because of how the other person is deciding to show up. How the other person decides to show up is not your fault or responsibility. And so, you can co-create the relationship dynamic you need by removing yourself from the situation, if need be, and asking for support if that is needed in order to exit.

Many of you fall into the trap of the ego of pointing the finger outside of yourself, but the true wisdom available to you through relationships is being able to more deeply look at yourself. What did you learn? How are you showing up? What are you allowing? What are you not? And so, we invite you to truly show up as the version of yourself you desire to be. If there are certain energies you desire in your relationship, or if you wish for dynamics to be a different way, show up in that vibration. Show up differently. Offer space for your partner to recalibrate. You both fall into routines, patterns, and behaviors that have been ingrained into your way of being over time, and so it will require a conscious choice to create new patterns. If you have primarily been using your right hand your whole life, it will require a conscious choice to then start using your left!

But how can you truly evaluate whether or not a relationship is resonant if you have not been holding the space to see if it can calibrate to your highest alignment and truth? Where are you deciding ahead of time? Where are you deciding for that other person? Where are you projecting limitations on them? Give people an opportunity to shift into their highest alignment. You do this by living this way yourself, holding that frequency, and then allowing energies to recalibrate if they are meant to. When you feel nonresonance, when you feel something is off, this is where you can learn more about yourself. *Am I communicating clearly? Have I been going through a shift, and so my needs and desires have shifted as well? Have I expressed and shared these shifts with my partner? How can I perceive this from a space of love and compassion for myself and my partner? If I am committed to clear communication and respect, how could I express this in the most loving way? How could I see from their perspective? How can I support my partner in better understanding me? How can I better understand my partner? Am I showing up for them the same way I desire them to show up for me? Where am I already expecting a no? Where am I expecting resistance, judgment, or rejection? Where am I choosing from fear instead of love?*

When it comes to making decisions about continuing a relationship, you could view it as a decision, or you could view it as commitment to your highest, most authentic self. Instead of putting pressure on a decision, you could orient from a commitment to living as the truest version of you, and then allowing others to make their own choices that will reveal if they are a vibrational match or not. This is about surrender. This is about releasing attachment. This is about trusting that what is for you will align with you, and that what is not meant to be in your reality at this time will fall away, creating space for what is in alignment to drop in. It is about allowing things to flow. It is about trusting rather than forcing. Where are you forcing? You cannot force another to change or to be different. How would that feel for you—to feel someone desiring you to be different? This is where you feel the energetic friction. The solution is simply to commit to being love, living as love, and showing up authentically. Communicate your desires. Show up with love and curiosity. Hold the frequency you desire in the relationship, and take action in alignment with that.

Every moment is a new beginning. You can shift yourself at any time. You can change a pattern, create a new habit, communicate differently, and show a different side of yourself. But you must choose this. When you choose to show up as the most authentic version of yourself, the truth will be revealed about who and what is a vibrational match, and who and what is not. From there, it is up to you to honor your truth. But again, many of you attempt to evaluate relationships when you are not showing up as the version of yourself that is in highest alignment, and so you get an inaccurate reading. What would it look like for you to set the tone, to set the frequency, and to offer a different way of being?

Relationship dynamics can absolutely change, but it requires conscious choice. It requires accountability and honesty. It requires the courage to look within instead of always pointing to someone or something else. You might find that in showing up differently, in showing up fully in your authenticity, inspiration, and excitement, in showing up as love, this offers space for an energetic shift in your partner. You might find they also start to shift into their most authentic self, the frequencies align again, and suddenly the meeting of these different frequencies is in highest alignment! You have co-created a completely different relationship container that has a completely different frequency. This is possible.

It is also possible that either party does not choose to align with their highest frequency, and this is their choice. The question is—how committed are you to your highest alignment? How committed are you to fully living as your most authentic self? How willing are you to claim divine partnership? To claim divine partnership will require releasing anything that is not. Where are you waiting for something in your reality to be different, yet you are not willing to make a change? If you are waiting for someone else to make a change, you are giving your power away. You are forgetting that you are a creator. Your happiness—your reality—does not depend on another. It is up to you to choose to live as your highest, most loving, most authentic self each day.

We understand that you will come across complications and doubts from the ego and logical mind. *How will this affect the rest of the family? What about finances, living situation, healthcare, and so on?* When you justify staying in situations that are not in highest alignment with logistics, this is where you are hiding. Remember, your reality will recalibrate to your frequency. And so, if releasing a relationship raises your vibration, your entire external reality will recalibrate to that higher frequency as well. Trust the voice of your soul, which can see the bigger picture. The ego will block you with fear, with how it will work out, with what will happen logistically. That is because the ego cannot always see the way out, and that is okay. Your soul is guiding you there. Your soul is nudging you to what is even better, even if your ego can't see it. When you choose from your soul, your logical mind recalibrates. The lens through which you see the world adjusts. It is from that adjusted lens and recalibrated frequency that you see and attract solutions you didn't before.

Notice where you are clouded with fear, and send love to these parts of yourself. We suggest making a clear list for yourself of all the fears, the doubts, the blocks, and the reasons why you think you "can't," even though you want to—bring it all to the surface. Let yourself see each thought. Sit with each thought. Ask yourself which are fear-based and which are love-based. Spend time with each. Which aspect of you is it connected to? What can you heal within yourself through exploring each aspect of your fear? As you go through each, is it really true that this cannot be recalibrated?

When you take the leap that is guided by your soul, your soul will also catch you, and carry you higher. When you choose to release that which is no longer serving you, when you release the anchors, when you decide to live as your truest self, when you decide to act in true, divine love for yourself, everything will also calibrate to that frequency. The universe is conspiring with you. There is a much bigger plan for you than your ego or logical mind can see. Will you trust your soul? This is about trusting yourself. This is about choosing your happiness. This is a choice only you can make. To not choose that is also a choice. The choices you make create your reality. Where are you staying because you believe you are not worthy of more? Because you think you will not find what you desire? Because you think nothing better will come along? This is where you are still in scarcity, still in lack, and still in illusion—still in the illusion of separation from Source, from divine love.

Remember who you truly are! Remember what is available for you. But you must make choices in alignment with the reality you wish to create if you wish to create it. As you make brave decisions that are aligned with love, watch as your reality recalibrates to be in alignment with that frequency. Watch how despite the worries, fears, and doubts you had about how it would all work out, it somehow just does. Choose in alignment with the frequency of miracles, and allow yourself to receive those miracles. The solutions can drop into your reality instantly, effortlessly, and in ways you could never plan. You are held. Things work out in mysterious ways.

But this is the key—you must commit to it working. If you are committed to it not working, if you are committed to expecting roadblocks and struggling, then that is the reality you are choosing. Claim what you are choosing. You can claim that you are choosing from love, and therefore it will work out in highest alignment for all, because you are holding the frequency of love. To anchor into highest love for yourself is also to do that for others, and that means holding that frequency so others have vibrational space to also live in this way, if they desire to. What frequency are you emitting? This is what many of you call "the example you're setting for others." If you wish for others to choose their own happiness, to be their most authentic selves, to claim what they are worthy and deserving of, to allow themselves to live as divine love, to allow themselves to receive divine love, then the best way to support them is to do this for yourself. We will call this the energetic trail that you leave. Your frequency is felt by others, whether or not they realize it. What do you wish to transfer to them? Love or fear? What energetic trail do you wish to leave behind?

Take responsibility for your energy field and for your frequency. This shows up in your thoughts, your actions, and your choices. It is choosing from love that supports the recalibration of all to that frequency. If you wish to get out of scarcity, fear, and heaviness, then you must choose from a different frequency. When you blame external circumstances for your unwillingness to make a shift, this is where you are in illusion, this is where you are not looking at yourself, this is where you are abdicating responsibility. You had certain beliefs that led to certain actions and choices that created the reality you are in now. You can choose different beliefs that lead to different actions and choices to create something different. You can always update the vibration. You can always communicate a different energetic signal. Your frequency is always shifting, and thus your reality is always shifting as well. Direct the energy in the way you desire if you desire something different. If you desire to feel differently, then you must choose that.

Remember that your feelings are your own responsibility, your vibration is your own responsibility, and any low-frequency emotions are indicating a deeper truth within you— something to be looked at. Low-frequency emotions are indicating that something is out of alignment—a belief, an action, a choice, a situation, or a relationship. Explore these frequencies. Explore anything that feels "off"—there is valuable information there that is leading you to a truth. When you uncover this truth, you illuminate a choice you can make to untangle that energy, to release that frequency, and allow yourself to fully rise. This is how you access freedom.

CHAPTER 45

CONSISTENT CHANGE

What is most consistent in this world is that everything is changing. You are always changing, and so are others. As you continue to learn, to grow, to explore, to shift, and to change, it is only natural that what is resonant for you will also shift and change. Your frequency shifts, so resonance shifts. Where are you punishing yourself for this? Where are you making yourself wrong for this? Give yourself permission to grow, to expand, and to change. Celebrate that you are committed to being your truest self, even as that changes. When a relationship is no longer resonant, this is a result of the frequencies shifting—why have you decided this is a bad thing? This is also about honoring the shifts and changes in others. Notice where you are projecting anger, resentment, fear, and judgment on each other for simply living as your most authentic selves, for following the natural flow of things, which is change!

You cannot prevent change. It is a false sense of security to wait until you feel like something will never change before committing to it. Let the commitment be to evolution, to exploration, to re-learning each other each and every day—that is the most beautiful part of the process! If things have gotten stagnant, stale, and boring, then are you truly showing up to the journey of fully learning each other? There is always more to learn and to explore. There are always new experiences to have and more aspects of yourselves to uncover—this is what keeps it exciting!

One partnership can offer infinite experiences, if you allow it to. This is why aligning based on soul resonance first is what will create a strong foundation moving forward. When you are aligned on a soul level with another, when you are entering the partnership as the most authentic versions of yourselves, the truest versions, the resonance is based on authenticity. Each iteration of you that activates throughout the course of the relationship will be based on that authentic frequency, and so while the iterations might shift and expand, the core frequency is the same, and this is what supports a longer, consistent partnership. But if the initial attraction was based on the ego, mind, logic, or an inauthentic version of one or both of you, the frequencies aligned based on the current iteration of you. As that shifts, you might not still be a vibrational match later on.

And so, if you are looking for a long-term relationship, the most important first step is to truly know and express yourself. Many enter into committed partnerships before they know themselves, and so they are not fully anchored into their authenticity or their truth, they adjust themselves at the beginning of the relationship to align with the other person, and they are not clear in what they truly desire.

Then, as they get to know themselves more and more through the relationship, they shift. They come in alignment with their truth, and there may or may not be vibrational resonance anymore. This is the experience for many at this time, as you are feeling called up to live fully in your authenticity. You are uncovering more of yourself, and you are recognizing where you entered into careers, relationships, and all sorts of situations and choices as an inauthentic version of yourself.

As you peel back the layers of who you really are, suddenly it's clear what is resonant with the real you, and what is not. Some of you might recognize that previous choices and situations were truly aligned for you at that time, but you shifted, while others might realize that it was, in fact, never really truly aligned. This is a great opportunity to learn more about yourself and your decision-making process. The things that are most fulfilling and long-lasting in your life will be chosen from a place of authenticity in that moment. Recognize that truth and authenticity can change, but what is true for you now? You might not know what will be true or most aligned for you forever, and you cannot wait around to figure that out, for it will be ever-changing. But you don't need to know, anyway! Focus on the present. The strongest foundation for you to move forward from is that of truth and authenticity. Trust that as you choose from that frequency, you add more momentum to it, and as that momentum builds, you are in the natural flow of creating a life that is aligned with your truth, aligned with your most authentic self, and aligned with divine love, even as different versions of your authenticity are unlocked and expressed throughout your lifetime.

Get to know yourself first, live in your truth first, find your authenticity first, and then you will have clarity on what you are looking for in a partnership and who you really are in a partnership. Fill your own cup first. Feel the way you wish to feel first. The energetic resilience will come easily from there. It is from this place that what you attract, and what you are attracted to, is most authentic to you and long-lasting. That does not necessarily mean that the relationship will never change. Again, you must simply honor the truth of the now. There might be a time when the contract is up, when the frequencies are no longer resonant, even if they once were, and even if they were for a long time. Where have you decided this is bad or wrong?

CHAPTER 46

CONSCIOUS UNCOUPLING

We would like to point out that you would perceive releasing relationships quite differently if your society wasn't designed in a way that made you feel so locked in. You are not truly "locked in" unless you allow yourself to be, but we recognize that as your society has shifted, many things have been set up to make it feel like quite an ordeal to detach. Again, you cannot let logistics stop you from living your truth. Would you rather move through some logistics and discomfort now, or live a lifetime of feeling stuck in lower frequencies? One is surrendering to your soul, while the other is surrendering to the system. One allows the lower frequencies to move through, while the other is choosing for those to consistently inform your reality.

We recognize that there has been much programming around "breakups" of all sorts, and divorce, and we invite you to see these from a different perspective. What if you released the projections, the judgments, and the stories attached to those things? Remember, your beliefs will shift your reality. Where and why have you decided divorce is wrong or bad? Where and why have you decided that breakups are messy, difficult, or unloving? Where and why have you decided that breakups indicate someone is wrong and someone is right? Where and why have you decided that something negative has to happen to justify the ending of a relationship? You need no justification—if it is not in highest alignment for you, it is not in highest alignment for all, and it is blocking everyone involved from becoming energetically available for their most aligned match. The judgments and beliefs you have about divorce and marriage are subjective. Moral judgments have been placed upon ending relationships that need not be your own to take on. Whose are those?

When a relationship is truly at its close, it is not serving anyone from highest love to stay in that relationship. That does not mean that any ending or closure is meant to be taken "lightly," so to speak—it should be viewed with the utmost respect, integrity, care, and love. However, it is important to evaluate the relationship with honesty, and notice where you are avoiding completing a relationship because of all the stories and judgments about it. Who are you really living for? Where are you still worried about external validation? The same way you can co-create the relationship, you can also co-create the ending of the relationship. Many of you refer to this as conscious uncoupling. This is a powerful new relationship template to fully activate on the planet. What would it look like to complete or release the relationship in a loving way on both sides, staying anchored in divine love, respect, and honor the whole way through? You can honor the relationship for its time, for its lessons, for its gifts. It truly is an incredible gift.

Closure is not a failure. It is a completion. It is a graduation. When you finish a level in your education, when you finish a book, when you complete a creative project, when you move into a new phase of your career, these can all be bittersweet endings. Just because there was the completion of a phase, a cycle, or a relationship does not mean it was for nothing. It was for everything! It is through the completion of relationships that some of your deepest learning and growth work is available. Notice how you shift through the process. What did you learn about yourself and others? Where did you show up authentically, with love, and where did you not? What lessons can you take from the relationship itself? For many, there can be powerful healing through conscious uncoupling.

The time and space after a relationship is complete is one of the most important spaces to truly let yourself sink into. It is a liminal stage where everything is recalibrating, and what the energy recalibrates to, what your new reality recalibrates to, will be dependent on the frequency you shift into through that liminal state. To shift into your highest, most authentic frequency, you must allow yourself to fully feel. Feel the sadness, the anger, the resentment, the frustration, the happiness, and the gratitude. Feel it all. Give yourself the space, the rest, and the nourishment that you need. It is like a child coming out of the womb, adjusting to this new incarnation. A mixture of emotions! Beautiful emotions. None of them are bad or wrong, all of them valuable information. Allow yourself to fully feel the emotions and let the frequencies move through without judgment, giving yourself and asking for whatever support you need and full nourishment. Act from highest love for yourself through the process. Through that process— that raw, messy, beautiful process—you will reach a state of clarity.

Many of you do not realize your energy becomes quite entangled with that of the other person in the relationship, and part of what happens when you uncouple is that the frequencies are starting to untangle as well. As that happens, recognize that so much of what you are feeling is not just yours, but also your previous partner's, and that of everyone else with an energetic attachment to the relationship, and the overall energetic chaos as the frequencies start to untangle. Allow yourself to fully release your emotions and to bring everything to the surface in that individual recalibration period in order to reach a state of clarity about what is yours and what is not. You might not fully know what is yours and what is not until the period of intense emotions moves through. During that time, you need not worry about whose it is, how, or why. Do not judge it or try to figure it out. Just feel it.

After those energies move through, you will start to see what is truly yours. You will start to rebuild your own energetic field and cleanse it from any frequencies that are no longer yours to carry. This is one of the most valuable lessons you receive on the other side of the relationship—*where did I get so energetically entangled that I was unclear on what was really mine, and how did that affect the relationship?* Reflecting on this allows you to move forward in new relationships with the awareness of how to keep your own field strong and clear, and how to relate without completely energetically entangling with another. Energetic enmeshment is often confused as love. They are not the same. We are sharing how to love and relate without energetic codependency.

As you move further into the liminal state and recognize what is really yours, this is also the period, which will continue to unravel over time, when you can fully reflect on and integrate the lessons. What were you meant to learn from that relationship? This is the crucial stage for vibrational shifts. This is why so many continue to attract different versions of the same energies—they do not take the time to fully integrate the lessons. Every relationship is teaching you crucial lessons unique to your contracts. Every relationship is preparing you. Are you taking the opportunities, or are you going to live out the same experiences over and over again? You will keep attracting the same energy until you fully integrate the lessons.

Integration is not just recognizing and thinking about the lessons—it is about making energetic shifts that reflect the wisdom learned. It moves from a thought to a knowing when it is embodied. True wisdom is embodied. When you become aware of what was available for you to learn and you integrate these lessons, your frequency recalibrates. You move forward in your life from this new vibration, and you naturally think, choose, and act differently. And so, the energy is different. It is from this different frequency that your field is able to fully energetically recalibrate to your highest alignment. If you have not fully integrated and embodied the lessons, your field will recalibrate back into the same frequency, and you will attract more of that same energy.

Again, the period after the completion of a relationship is one of the most fruitful periods of self-growth for many of you. You feel many emotions intensely, and some of this pain is in fact the growing pains of the heart. The heart breaks and rebuilds to be stronger, to hold more love, to receive more love, with more knowledge, with a greater energetic capacity, with more power. Those growing pains are not comfortable, but you must stretch to grow. It is sometimes the situations that hurt the most that impact you the most profoundly, that teach you your greatest lessons—these get your attention. They force you to look more deeply. You cannot avoid the pain. Emotions are powerful indicators, and underneath them you will find there is so much to learn about yourself—things you never expected.

When you complete the relationship, we see it is an ending to that specific relationship container. What we mean by this is that just because a relationship ends does not mean love ends. What it means to live as love and from love is to always be acting from divine love, and this carries through in your uncoupling. In fact, this is a powerful test of your energetic resilience—do you uphold the frequency of love through the ending of the relationship? Upholding the frequency does not mean not feeling low-frequency emotions. What is authentic is from love. You can feel a vast variety of emotions and still act and speak from a place of love for that other person.

It is not that divine love ends, it is simply that it manifests and is expressed differently. The divine love can hold firm, yet the relationship shifts form. The relationship itself might shift from a romantic partnership to a friendship, or to no friendship. There is no right or wrong—but what frequency is the choice coming from? For many, remaining present in each other's lives might not be resonant or healthy—but this does not mean you must deviate from the frequency of love. Again, divine love does not necessitate commitment, presence, overlooking anything, or excusing anything. You can uncouple, have no further contact, uphold your boundaries, and still be aligned with divine love through the whole process.

We will also point out that the ending of the relationship container does not necessarily mean it cannot be rebuilt. In fact, many of you who want to transform your current relationships will find more success in a relationship with that "same" person if you complete the current relationship container, realign yourself, and enter a new relationship with that person, where you are both anchored into your authenticity, where you are co-creating a relationship container that is of the frequency that feels most aligned for you. There are times when you can adjust the painting, and other times when it is more aligned to put the canvas aside and simply start anew. Perhaps the concept is still resonant, but the execution needed adjustment—clearer inspiration came through! We point this out because sometimes it is not aligned timing to be with someone. Sometimes you need to surrender to a period of truly understanding and learning yourselves before the relationship container could be aligned with what you both desire. But what is truly for you will not miss you.

Closing a relationship container does not have to mean you cannot have a relationship with that person again, from our perspective. If you are meant to, your frequencies will meet, but then you have an opportunity to co-create what is truly most aligned. Remember, choose from love, not fear. If you are afraid that releasing something means you might lose it forever, you are not trusting vibrational resonance. To relate from divine love is not to hold tightly to the things you desire and force them to stay in your reality. To relate from divine love is to release, and then allow what is truly meant to float alongside you and to vibrate with you to naturally do so. It is vibrational resonance that will keep things in your field without you having to hold on so tightly. What a relief—to see the truth of what is fully aligned, rather than cling to a false sense of control and always wonder who or what would naturally be in your reality if you were flowing instead of forcing!

And so, we do not view breakups as something to fear. We will remind you that you have the power to transmute the energy and beliefs about breakups. You have the power to shift them into alignment with the frequency of uncoupling with love. Notice if you are able to uphold your frequency of divine love through the process. You need not worry if the other does, for that is their choice. Remember that on the other side of the lowest lows are the highest highs. Remember that when you release what is no longer resonant, this creates space for something better to come in, if you allow it to. Allow yourself to fully learn, receive, and integrate your lessons. Use the transition period to clear and then fortify your energy field. Every time a relationship is completed, there is a massive energetic upgrade available to you—a massive shift in your frequency available to you—because these are some of the most potent experiences for you to learn more about yourself and to more fully align with your authenticity.

There is no need to judge your soul contracts or when frequencies are no longer resonant. It is from your reactions and judgments that you can recognize where you are still living from programming, still living from wounds, still living from fears, still dipping into lower frequencies to cope, instead of viewing the completion from an energy of divine love. The process of death and rebirth is quite natural for you. It is the natural flow of your world. There are death and rebirth cycles all throughout nature, including you. There are death and rebirth cycles all throughout your life, with the completion of cycles offering openings for new energies. Otherwise, it would be the same the whole way through. How boring would that be!

If you never shift cycles, you won't experience the greatest level of soul evolution in this incarnation, and you won't get to know all the aspects of your most authentic self! Sometimes these death and rebirth cycles occur in the relationship containers themselves. Sometimes the death and rebirth occurs inside the relationship container, and sometimes the container is meant to come to a close. Your relationship with the completion of a relationship will mirror your relationship with death itself. Remember, you can shift any relationship, if you so desire.

CHAPTER 47

RELATIONSHIP CONTAINERS

We will return to the topic of different relationship containers, and remind you that we do not see things from the perspective of better than or worse than, right or wrong. We explore things from an energetic perspective, and offer suggestions based on what keeps your frequency high and aligns you with your divine truth. There are different relationship containers that exist, and all serve their purposes for different individuals, different lessons, and different seasons. It is all about—what is most authentic for you at this time? This will be different for each of you, as you each have a unique frequency.

But we will ask—where are you deciding what is most authentic for you from your ego rather than your soul? We bring this up because the way in which you relate to different relationship containers will teach you much about yourself. Notice where any particular container triggers you—what is this illuminating within you? Where do you have judgment toward any container? Marriage, long-term commitment, monogamy, polyamory, and so on are examples of different choices, and the key is what is most authentic for you, and what feels most aligned with your truth. What we will offer, however, is that if you are choosing a container out of avoidance, or because of what is authentic for someone else, this will lower your frequency, and there is something else to look at underneath this.

Beyond that, we will also point out that the frequency of commitment in a partnership is actually an energetic door that opens up a deeper connection to your essence as Source itself. Where you are afraid of commitment is where you are afraid to see clearly in the mirror, is where you might be afraid of your own power, is where you might be afraid to be deeply seen, to be deeply loved. When you are in the energy of commitment to yourself, you will desire this to be reflected in your relationship. And it is commitment to another that allows space for depth, for growth, for greater mirroring, and for deeper connection to Source. If you go on twenty first dates, how deep do you really go with each? If you go on one first date and nineteen after with the same person, assuming they are an aligned match, this allows for greater depth in connection. It is this depth in connection that allows you to see more aspects of yourself, and deeper aspects of yourself. It is this depth in connection that deepens your connection to love itself.

When your energy is focused in one direction, momentum flows, and so the energy expands. When your energy is dispersed, there will be less momentum and expansion in any single direction. Distraction disperses your energy, which dulls your power. Focusing on anything intently allows the energy to concentrate and to expand, and your results will be amplified in that direction. To master anything, you must focus on it and concentrate your energy in that direction. If you are trying to learn basketball by playing a different sport every week, how do you expect to step into your mastery? When you focus your energy on mastering basketball, you will reach a point of mastery where you might get into more advanced techniques, or you might choose to explore another sport as well. But even if your skills are so ingrained in your muscle memory that you choose another sport, there will still be choices to be made about how you spend your time. Depending on the level of mastery and energetic capacity, one might find that as they spend more time mastering the other sport, their basketball skills dull a bit, and it takes a little practice to fully reactivate their skillset to the level it once was. Another person might have a different experience—perhaps their mastery is deeply ingrained, and they could set the ball down for years and still maintain that exact level of mastery when they pick the ball up again. We would say the former is more common than the latter. There are many possibilities, and so it comes down to honoring your truth, your energetic capacity, your goals, and your desires. There is no right or wrong. There is no formula. The answer is in following your own highest alignment, what is in alignment with your goals through the connection, and what you desire out of a partnership.

When it comes to anchoring fully into your highest vibration, focusing your energy in alignment with this will be the most efficient path there, vibrationally, because the energy is not dispersed. The energy is concentrated. This is where committed partnerships allow deep opportunities to know and understand yourself, to fully give and receive divine love, and to connect to Source itself on a deeper level through the connection itself, because the energy is concentrated, in alignment with divine love, in a focused direction.

Commitment in a relationship, as we see it, is a commitment to your growth, a commitment to not running away from yourself, a commitment to not avoiding when things are reflected back to you, a commitment to never forgetting your inherent wisdom and abilities when challenges arise, and a commitment to not running away from uncomfortable conversations. It is a commitment to showing up to the opportunities that allow you to grow, to expand, to remember your own power, to remember your wisdom, and to deepen your inner trust and knowing. That is what you are truly committed to. Commitment to learning, understanding, and supporting another of true vibrational resonance, who you relate to from the frequency of divine love, mirrors your own commitment to learning, understanding, and supporting yourself. This commitment is to learning, understanding, and supporting through every iteration and cycle. This commitment is to enjoying the journey!

If you are getting bored in a relationship, you might reflect on where you are bored with yourself. Are you growing? Are you expanding? Are you learning about yourself? If you are stagnant, the relationship will feel stagnant. You wonder how to keep the spark alive—keep the spark alive with yourself! As you keep exploring new aspects of yourself and sharing them with your partner, new energies, dynamics, experiences, and conversations will naturally come forward. When you are curious with yourself, this curiosity naturally flows into your relationship. You will naturally be curious to understand and learn your partner more deeply. When you are both in alignment with expansion, there is always more to uncover! Bringing new things into the relationship and keeping things exciting is not a chore or unnatural when you are naturally in this energy yourself. It is when you connect with and embrace your own multidimensionality that you will naturally see this and get curious about this in your partner, and it is from this place that things always stay exciting!

If you feel you have lost the spark, where have you lost the spark within yourself? You must be inspired yourself, first! Divine love is playful! It is fun! It is pure joy! It is creative! When you anchor into this frequency, let the play flow, let the fun flow, and let the creativity flow. Create together! It is through play and fun that you will reconnect with your truest essence—joy! Wherever you're taking things a bit too seriously, you can always show up with a fresh perspective! Where are you not living your truth or authenticity? If you are living out of alignment with your authentic self, this will lead to fatigue and frustration, and that will get carried into the relationship. Light yourself up first, get inspired yourself first, get curious yourself first, explore new things, and share this in your partnership.

It is living authentically, honoring the shifts and changes, the expansion, and frequency shifts themselves that keep the excitement alive. There is always more to learn, more to explore, and more opportunities to see different parts of yourselves. Although you might think change is what breaks many relationships apart, is what creates the vibrational gap, it is also the very same thing that keeps soul resonant relationships growing, thriving, expanding, and aligned with endless excitement and curiosity.

CHAPTER 48

SEXUAL CHEMISTRY

We will continue our discussion about divine love and romantic relationships by exploring sexual relationships and sexual chemistry. There are certain frequencies that will meet, and when coming together, activate the frequency of creation. When those vibrations come together, they activate something that is the doorway to Source itself. While the topic of sex could have its own entire text of the same length, what we will say is that most of your views on sex as we see it have been quite distorted. We see sexual relations as the most potent form of energey exchange. Sexual energy is direct access to your divine power source and flow of life force energy, so it is no wonder that efforts have been made to disconnect you from it. Some ways this has occurred have been through normalizing casual sexual relationships, normalizing sexual interactions from an energy out of alignment with the frequency of divine love, and, on the other end of the spectrum, looking down upon sex and self-pleasure practices and attempting to make them taboo topics.

When you recognize sex as a potent energetic exchange, you might see things differently. You exchange energy simply by thinking about or being around people. To allow someone access to your physical vessel is direct access to the most powerful and also most vulnerable parts of you. Who are you allowing to access this potency, this power, this creativity, this part of you? What many of you do not realize are the longer lasting energetic repercussions of sexual exchange. The normalization of casual sexual exchange is one of the direct causes of ongoing health issues, constant fatigue, anxiety, depression, mental illness, and so on. There are other factors, of course, but energetically this is one of the ways you disconnect from your inner source and dim your power the most. You can rebuild and reactivate this.

Orgasm is a direct pathway to Oneness, to the Source, to all that is. It is a beautiful, sacred, divine experience. In this experience, the moment when you are at your highest frequency of pleasure, of ecstasy, or connecting with Source—this is where creation happens. You understand this as the creation of another being, for example, but that is not the only thing that can be created here. The energy, the intention, the thoughts that are brought into sexual energy exchange, that are brought into orgasms, are a direct reflection of what is created in that space. If someone were to give you a magical object from which you could create anything, how would you relate to the responsibility that came with that power?

When you are exchanging sexual energy, you are exchanging that aspect of you—the central point of your power of creation—with that other person. Who do you wish to share that with? And who do you wish to receive that from? This is one of the most common ways your energy fields get dulled and weakened, where you experience leaky energetic boundaries, where you feel exhausted and heaviness, where your magnetism is dulled, where you take on other people's energy. When you look at all of the energy you are carrying for other people, all of the emotions you might feel from energetic connections with other people, and how that occurred, perhaps the most important place to look is sexual energy exchange. As powerful as an orgasm is when it comes to creation, there are also things that can dull its power, so to speak. There are many practices you can use to build your sexual energy, your inner power, and this is your direct access point to your spiritual gifts, your intuitive gifts, everything turning online, manifestation, a clear path to supercharging your energy field and connecting to Source itself, when accessed in alignment with divine love.

As an extension of Source, you also carry the power of creation, and those creative abilities are their most potent through the experience of an orgasm anchored in divine love. Sexuality has been shamed throughout much of your history as a way of keeping people out of their power, and then it was distorted as another way of lowering people's vibrations and their overall magnetism. If you wish to fully step into your highest frequency, explore your relationship with your sexual connection. It is a beautiful thing! This is about pleasure. This is about love. This is about feeling. This is about inspiration. This is about creativity. This is about your connection with your body. This is about trust. This is about surrender. This is about flow. This is about freedom. It is an access point to Source itself. But you can choose whether to honor your sexual energy, build it, cultivate it, and direct it toward your desires that are in highest alignment with divine love, or you can deplete it, neglect it, and direct it unintentionally toward that which you do not desire. Everything in the physical has an energetic root, and the depletion and distortion of your sexual energy is in fact one of the most common energetic roots of many health issues in your society, particularly much of the fatigue and stress. So many of you give away your power without even recognizing it, and then wonder why you feel all out of sorts. Others avoid their sexuality and sexual connection, and wonder why they feel exhausted and uninspired.

When you recognize that sex is a potent energy exchange, a portal created between you and the other to connect directly with oneness—with Source itself—and to truly create with clear intention, do you view it differently? When you show up with full love, honor, and respect for yourself, when you treat yourself with divine love, when you recognize your own divinity and sacredness, when you recognize your own power and how magnetic you are, do you think about sexual relationships differently? You will experience sex and orgasms differently when you are embodying your most authentic frequency. You will, in fact, experience orgasms quite differently when the entire connection is anchored into the vibration of divine love. When both people are anchored into this frequency, when the relationship container itself is of this vibration, this is the most potent frequency to experience sex from. This is a direct access point to full body orgasms, to channeling this energy to supercharge, balance, and heal your energy bodies and physical bodies, to cosmic orgasms that connect you directly with the divine.

Would you take someone through the portal to the divine with you who did not honor you? Who did not respect you? Who was not a vibrational match for the experience itself? It is at the point of orgasm where you will find a clear access point to your powers of creation, but this opening also allows you to absorb other energies more deeply. And so, who are you exchanging sexual energy with? What is the frequency you're bringing into the experience? When you see sexual exchange as the divine portal that it is, when you understand the energetic repercussions of the exchange, you might honor it differently. You might appreciate it differently. You might take care of your vessel differently and relate to it differently. What would it look like for the frequency of divine love to be threaded through your relationship with your sexual organs, your sexual energy, with sex itself? Who do you wish to connect to oneness with, and from what energy? If you knew you could create anything, who would you wish to co-create with? What do you think about before and during sex? What is your intention going into sex? All of this will be mirrored in what you create from that energy exchange—most of you do not realize this.

Your sexual energy is precious, sacred magic. Orgasm is a divine act of magic. Who are you sharing that with? How are you sharing that? Why are you sharing it in the way you are, with the person you are? Again, there is no right or wrong, but if we are exploring divine love from an energetic perspective, the discussion would be incomplete without this, because one of the most common ways that you are not living as divine love and from divine love is in how you relate to sex— your direct connection to Source, to Oneness, to God, to the divine. This is your direct portal to creation.

If you are committed to living from your highest frequency, you must explore the energy leaks, you must explore where you are forgetting your power, you must explore where you are abdicating responsibility, you must explore where you are not honoring your divinity, you must explore where you are not living from love, you must explore where you are living unconsciously, and you must explore where you are taking on low-frequency energies that are not your own. Sexual energy exchange is the most relevant place to look. When you know that your sexual energy is your magic, when you know it is the energetic flow of your divinity, you might relate to it differently, and you might relate to your vessel differently. When you truly honor yourself, you will honor your sexual energy, and when you truly honor your own sexual energy, you will also naturally honor that of others.

There is so much magic available to you, and one of the direct portals to this is through orgasm—this point of creation. It is a point of creation whether or not you wish to have a child. It is far beyond this. It is the most potent amplification of and exchange of energies. The reason why, on a core level, you crave connection is because you crave oneness. You crave divine love. You crave Source itself. And orgasm is a direct access point to this magic. Sexual energy is the flow of this magic. But the true magic can only be revealed when you recognize the portal for what it is.

From this understanding, you might also come to appreciate celibacy in a new way. Again, there is no right or wrong, but we would like to highlight the energetics of these choices. When you understand the true power of sexual energy, that this is Source moving through you, that this is your creation and manifestation ability flowing through you, your life force flowing through you, you might honor your orgasm and sexual practices more deeply. How you protect, cultivate, and activate your sexual energy is your choice, and might shift throughout your life. But you will not fully know yourself if you do not know yourself in connection to sexuality. One form of honoring your sexual energy, cultivating it, and respecting it might also include abstaining from sexual relations for a period of time. When done from a place of divine love for yourself, for your vessel, for your magic, this can be a powerful way to replenish and recharge, to amplify your energetic potency, and to raise your vibration. Meanwhile, others might use intentional, divine orgasm to do the same. Intention is everything. Part of fully knowing yourself as a sexually energetic being is exploring your relationship with sexual energy exchange, and without sexual energy exchange.

When it comes to ascension as individuals and as a collective, we see your relationship with sex shifting as a whole. It is where you can access some of your most powerful gifts, but also where you have been unknowingly shutting it off. It is all in how you choose to relate to it. Remember, when you live as divine love, when you choose as divine love, you are anchored into love, respect, integrity, and authenticity. You are focused and clear in your frequency, your intentions, and how and where you direct and concentrate your energy. Approach sexual energy exchange with this same frequency, and watch as your entire reality recalibrates.

To complete our exploration of sexuality and of different types of relationships, we will also touch on different genders and sexes in love. We see, vibrationally, divine love as divine love. When energies connect vibrationally and the spark is lit of romantic, divine love, this is beyond sex or gender. When energies connect vibrationally and the spark of divine love is felt in the context of friendship or family, this is beyond sex or gender. Love is love. As the planet continues to shift vibrationally, you will find that your understanding of these also shifts drastically. You will also find that as more step into their most authentic selves, whatever has been "normalized" in your community will deteriorate. At your highest frequency as a collective, there will be no norms. You will be co-creating the relationships you desire, that are in highest alignment with you. Living in the belief that love must look one way is where you are still running off of programs and conditioning. It is where you are unintentionally living in limitations. Love has no limits. It is healing, it is transformational, it is powerful, it is within all, and it moves through all. It is vibrational, not logical. It moves beyond any rational understanding. That is why it is so magical.

CHAPTER 49

UNLEARNING

As we near the end of our discussion on divine love, we would like to point out some of the most common energetic blocks in relationships of all sorts, in terms of allowing yourself to fully give and receive the divine love that is available within you and for you. We offer these examples for you to tune into what is vibrationally resonant for you. They may or may not resonate. Simply seeing the option can spark the realization of what was hidden subconsciously, and when it is brought to conscious awareness, you can make any shifts that are in highest alignment for you.

Where we will begin is with conditioning, fears, and wounds from your relationship with your parents. Children are very sensitive, intuitively and energetically open beings, and they learn about the world and relationships through what is modeled to them. They pick up far more than most realize. Because of that, their parents or guardians are typically the most influential models when it comes to relationships. The dynamics between their parents are typically what they are around most, what they see the most, and how they learn to relate. And so, it is from parents that children will learn what they believe to be "normal" in terms of communication, in terms of expression, in terms of boundaries, and in terms of love. The dynamics that are picked up are in what they see occurs between parents, the dynamics between their parents and other people who are not their parents, and also the dynamics between the parents and themselves, as the child.

You are wired to remember intense experiences. Moments that feel like a blip, easily forgotten, to an adult can create a deep impression on a child that might last a lifetime. Children feel pure energy, pure emotion, while most adults contextualize the energy and emotions they feel through their thoughts, logic, and conditioning. Children receive that pure emotion and pure energy without the conditioning, logic, or energetic armor to block it. This is not about blame or judgment—all plays its role, and these impressions are typically unintentional. It is part of moving through the world, part of the human experience of growing up. You chose your family, your parents, and your contracts that would provide you with the experiences and opportunities for your highest growth and learning.

It is also your relationship with your parents from a young age that informs much of your relationship with masculine energy and feminine energy, which, again, are outside of sex or gender. These energies are related to boundaries, accountability, direct communication, structure, giving, receiving, rest, intuition, creativity, play, and so on. But the child often interprets them to be connected with the idea of "father" or "mother," because they learn these energies and see these energies modeled from their parents. This is also how the child learns certain roles parents might play—in the family unit, in relation to each other, and in relation to the children. The child interprets based on the information they have, unaware that so many other individuals and family units operate differently. You know what you know.

One of the most powerful growth practices you can engage in as an adult that will shift all relationship dynamics in your life is to spend time exploring what you "learned" at a young age—intentionally or unintentionally—from your parents. Again, this is not just about what you were told, but also what you concluded, thought, assumed, or understood based on what you saw and felt. You might also extend this exploration practice out to other relationships you have had—friendships, romantic relationships, teachers, extended family, or colleagues. But it is in what you learned from the relationship with your parents, and often siblings, where you will find the root of many energy knots—where the seed was planted that then created a domino effect leading to certain expectations, assumptions, beliefs, behaviors, and energetic dynamics in relationships that came after.

The exploration can begin with your birth story, and then move into how you felt as a child, what you saw your parents' relationship to be like, and what you learned about what was "good" and "bad" and "right" and "wrong" in terms of behavior. As an adult, you can see this from a neutral perspective, understanding that good, bad, right, and wrong are all subjective, are rooted in a lower-frequency perspective, are still judgments out of alignment with your highest self. The point of this process is not to judge, but rather to observe what was learned.

You might ask the younger you, *did I feel safe to express my needs? How did I receive love? How did I learn love was expressed? When was I reprimanded? Did I feel safe to express myself? What did I learn that success meant? How much affection was I given? How much affection was shown in general? What did I learn was a "good" relationship? How were boundaries modeled for me? In what ways did I feel I was not allowed* to have boundaries? In what ways did I feel suppressed? What made me feel heard and seen? When did I not feel heard and seen? What made me feel loved? How did my parents show me love? How did they show each other (or their partners) love? What did I perceive to be a burden to my parents? What did I learn was the role of each parent in the relationship? What did I learn was the role of each parent in raising me? What did I learn my role was? What was I not allowed to do? What was I praised for? What did I feel judged for? When did I feel more than enough? When did I not? What did I learn was normal communication? How did we communicate? These are just a few valuable questions to begin with in this exploration.

From there, you can start to unpack your relationship with masculine and feminine energy. Both of these energies are within you individually, and these energies will show up in your relationship dynamics. What did you learn masculine energy looked like or felt like? What do you think of when you think of masculine energy? What did you learn feminine energy looked like or felt like? What do you think of when you think of feminine energy? When you reflect on your parents, what felt secure, stable, grounded, trustworthy, and safe? What did holding space look like? When you reflect on your parents, what felt soft, compassionate, caring, intuitive, and creative? What did you learn about rest? What did you learn about play? What did you learn about the balance of doing and being? What did you learn productivity meant? What felt chaotic? What felt uncontrolled? What felt dominating or aggressive? It is from these questions you can start to explore what you learned about masculine and feminine energy, and from here you can start to pull apart what is illusion and what is not.

Many of you push away divine love because you were modeled something that did not feel safe, stable, or secure, and so you either expect that, or fear you do not know how to create something else. Many of you unintentionally push away divine love because you do not feel safe to receive. You might push away the voice of your intuition because you believe the feminine is chaotic, naive, or gullible. You might avoid boundaries in relationships because you felt you could not have them as a child or were reprimanded if you tried to implement them. This can lead to people-pleasing tendencies and low energetic resilience as an adult. You might struggle with clear, direct communication because you were not modeled clear communication as a child, you did not feel safe to express your feelings, or you were taught to keep your feelings inside. Through exploring your relationship with your parents, you can start to unravel your beliefs about masculine and feminine energy, where you have unintentionally disconnected from the empowered forms of these within yourself, and where you are expecting the disempowered forms of these from others. Notice where you are expecting competition, jealousy, guilt trips, shame, judgment, rejection, or abandonment from others.

You can also start to unpack what your fears are about entering a relationship to begin with. Remember, what happened before does not have to happen again. To experience it, yourself or through witnessing another, is an opportunity to learn the lessons that will allow you to make the energetic shifts that will create something different. Understanding what dynamics do not work is a powerful way to get clear on the dynamics you do desire to create in a relationship. You get to co-create the relationship you truly desire, the relationship that is a container for divine love. You do not have to have already experienced it with another person to co-create it—you simply have to anchor into the vibration, available to you any moment you choose.

Through exploring your relationship with your parents and between your parents, you can bring to light any underlying expectations or assumptions you have about how relationships work, how long they last, where they have to be difficult, where they involve conflict, where they will inevitably end, where love is earned, where worth is proven, and so on. Dive into the pile of illusions and bring them to the surface. View them from the perspective of divine love, and this will shine the light brightly on the illusions. From here, you can transmute those beliefs into divine love and truth, and you can reprogram your expectations. If you are expecting what you previously experienced or saw, you can rewrite the story and choose differently. You already experienced that, and so you can choose to make an energetic shift to realign with something else. Notice where you are still living out of wounds from a younger version of yourself—feeling unworthy, feeling undeserving, judging yourself, fearing judgment, fearing rejection, fearing abandonment, believing you must do something to earn love, feeling you must prove yourself, fear of being loved, or fear that you will never find it.

You don't need to look far to find it when you recognize it has been within you all along. It has moved through you all along. When you choose to embody the frequency and to act on the frequency, you are the frequency, and more flows your way. The fear of being loved— what is it you are really afraid of? Is it divine love you fear, or do you fear an experience someone else called love but was really something else? Notice where your fears derive from, what they really are, and if they are truly serving you. What you fear in your subconscious is a frequency in your field, and you get to transmute those frequencies to be in alignment with what you wish to experience and attract. It is important to recognize these fears and limiting beliefs so you can remind yourself of the divine truth and release the illusions.

You are love. You are endlessly worthy and deserving of love. You need not do anything to earn it. Does it serve you to fear judgment, rejection, and abandonment? Are judgment, rejection, and abandonment worth fearing? Or are they just one perspective of viewing a vibrational mismatch being communicated in a low-frequency way? What stories did you create about yourself when someone else chose fear over love? When someone else chose out of alignment with their highest self? What projections are you taking on from others that are not yours to carry? And so, it is what you learned unintentionally from dynamics modeled to you, including that of your parents, that informs what you believe is to be expected in and of relationships, what you fear in relationship dynamics, and what you believe is possible in relationships. When you are unintentionally operating from these fears, from these wounds, and from this pain, you create self-fulfilling prophecies, you interpret situations through the lens of these wounds, and you stay disconnected from your essence as divine love.

You get to write your own story. Notice the areas within you that need nurturing, love, and care. Tend to them. Anywhere you did not feel loved or cared for as a child, if not yet explored, you will unintentionally seek to be fulfilled through your relationships. This is a misdirected desire. Your partner cannot and is not meant to fill the role of your parent. This is your opportunity to give yourself what you felt your parents did not. This is your opportunity to give yourself what you desire—to source it from within, to source it from your direct connection to the divine.

Let yourself be supported! Let yourself be loved, seen, heard, and energized by the divine within—by the endless love of your soul. It is where you are unintentionally desiring a hole to be filled by another that you are still operating from lack, from scarcity. This is disconnected from abundance, from your endless supply of love within. And so, as you speak to these tender parts of yourself and uncover what it is you truly crave and need, you can give this to yourself, allow Source to give this to you, and allow divine love to do its healing work. From there, you remember your wholeness, your power, and your magic. From there, you can enter a relationship from a healed place, from a whole place, and from a place where you can accurately evaluate what is a vibrational match on a soul level and what is not, rather than what is a vibrational match for the ego and what is not.

CHAPTER 50

THE MOST COMMON ENERGETIC BLOCKS IN RELATIONSHIPS

From this understanding, the rest of the common blocks start to be revealed—the main one being, as we mentioned previously, communication. If there is one thing that will shift all of your relationship dynamics into higher alignment, into authenticity, it is clear communication. It is from unclear communication that conflict, drama, expectations, assumptions, and disappointments derive. You will find that far more relationships find flow and understanding from clear communication, and that the truth of relationships is revealed far earlier on when all parties are communicating clearly and authentically. To build an honest relationship in integrity, you must communicate authentically. If you are not communicating clearly and authentically, is this truly operating from the frequency of divine love?

It is only through clear communication that you can open the space for truth to be revealed, and it is truth that forms the strongest foundation for any relationship. It is through clear communication that you can express your desires, be clear in what you are looking to co-create, be honest about past experiences and how they might inform your current emotions, be honest about what values and principles are important to you, what you desire for your reality, and so on. When this is all on the table, there is clarity about if there is alignment or not. If you desire someone to be able to truly love you on a soul level, you must show them who you are on a soul level.

Another aspect of authentic, clear communication is showing up as your most authentic self! Share the truest version of yourself, not an adjusted one. It serves no one to dull yourself down or to adjust your frequency in any way. This will lead to an unclear perception of you. How can you really know if you like a book if you only read one page? That is what it is to only show a part of yourself, or to adjust yourself. Communicate clearly about your fears instead of projecting them onto your partner. Communicate about how things make you feel instead of expecting someone to read your mind. Communicate about how things feel so all perspectives can be brought to the table, and so you can see the true meaning behind things with compassion and understanding, instead of stories and illusions you might be holding onto from the past. Communication requires sharing and listening. Clear communication requires knowing yourself, knowing your own needs, and knowing your own boundaries—you can clearly express what you know.

Here is another one of the biggest energetic blocks to attracting in the most aligned match—not truly knowing yourself. To know yourself allows you to show up authentically, and from here you attract in an authentic, soul-aligned match. If you are always in partnership, it will be difficult to truly know what is yours and what is not—your interests, your emotions, your beliefs. It is time in your own energetic field that allows you to truly do the vibrational work, the energetic fortification and exploration, to become anchored into your authentic truth and allow yourself to enter a relationship from a whole place, instead of codependence, energetic enmeshment, and confusion. Do not be afraid to have energetic requirements. These are what allow you to uphold your frequency, and this is how you maintain the frequency of divine love the whole way through.

We invite you to notice how much of what has been normalized in your society is an addiction to adrenaline, to stories, and to instant gratification. Many of you unintentionally attract and create patterns where there is back and forth, push and pull, unclear communication, disrespectful behavior, and drama. If you are used to this, it will be familiar, and therefore more comfortable to your ego, and you might unintentionally attract it in. But is that what you really desire? It will require you to stop operating from your ego and to start leading from your heart if you truly want to experience divine partnership and divine love. You can keep playing games, but do not be surprised when you attract more in. You can keep looking for instant gratification, but do not be surprised when you are left unfulfilled, when you realize that the fleeting moment of a false sense of love never quite satisfies the desire deep in your soul.

Notice where you are feeling disconnected from purpose, from mission, and from your highest self. You get to choose something different, but it will require you to choose to live from the frequency you wish to create in your life. When you do, you will realize which habits, behaviors, and perspectives are not really that of your highest self, but of your ego, of your inner child, of the scared, hurt, version of you, of the illusions within you, of those around you who are not fulfilled themselves. While it is your choice whether or not you wish to align with divine love, to experience it, and to live as it, it is the path to your purpose. What you seek on a core level is love, because that is what you are. That is your truth. To be fully immersed in divine love is to live in full connection with oneness, with Source, with the infinite realm of possibility. It is pure ecstasy. You are an extension of this.

Fully activating this connection is what reconnects you to your inner knowing, your intuition, your inner gifts, your power, your joy, your divinity, your inspiration, your excitement, your ecstasy, and your most expanded self. Will you choose this? It might feel easier in the moment to choose from your ego, to perceive from your ego, and to go back to old patterns, but is it really? Is it truly easier, or is it just automatic? It is not easy to live your life out of alignment. It is not easy to live a life where you are always searching, seeking, and craving more. It is not easy to live a life where you feel the deep knowing within that more is available to you, but you keep feeling unfulfilled no matter what you try. This happens when what you are trying is out of alignment with divine love. This happens when what you are trying is from your ego. This happens when you are searching for something externally when it is right inside of you— but you must recognize it.

You will not recognize divine love in a relationship until you recognize it within yourself. You will not feel divine love in a relationship until you feel it within yourself. You will not feel the depth of love in a divine partnership until you see and love the depths of yourself.

Connect with divine love itself, and become familiar with the frequency. This is in your connection to Source, in your connection with yourself. Choose to act from that frequency rather than your ego, your fear, your conditioning, and your automatic processing. Choose to act from that conscious place of divine love instead of what has been normalized in connection to what you have called love but is really obligation, commitment, lust, addiction, and infatuation. It is all up to you. It is all within you. What frequency will you act from?

CHAPTER 51

THE DIVINE
LOVE IN YOU

Divine love is your truth. It is a driving force because it is what makes you you. You seek it because you know, on a soul level, it is the frequency that aligns you directly with your truth, your truest essence, with oneness, with Source itself. You, as an extension of Source, are from love. It is home. It is what created you. It is what naturally flows through you. It is the infinite source of healing, of power, of transformation, of possibility, of pleasure, of oneness. It is what you yearn for, because you yearn to live as your highest, purest expression—love. When you are aligned with love, your reality recalibrates to this frequency. Is this not what you all seek? Many of you spend your entire lives searching for it, when it was right within you all along. All along, it was recognizing it within, nurturing it within, and acting from it that naturally allows more of it to appear in your external reality. But you must choose it. You must uphold it. You must commit to it, which is really committing to that part of you. It is choosing your highest expression.

Love is truth. Are you willing to choose truth over illusion? Are you willing to choose responsibility over avoidance? Are you willing to choose soul over ego? Are you willing to choose oneness over separation? Are you willing to choose authenticity over fleeting moments of instant gratification? Are you willing to choose love over fear? Everything comes down to choice, and this is the power you have. You always have the power to choose differently. You always have the power to perceive differently. If this text has unlocked anything for you, we hope it is the understanding of divine love itself. We hope this text has dissolved your confusion about what that means, and we hope it has shed light on where you might have been unintentionally operating from what you were told love is, rather than what you know it is, on a soul level. Your soul is always guiding you with love, to love. Your intuition is guiding you to it. Your soul is guiding you to a life filled with it, but will you be brave enough to choose it? To choose divine love? To shatter the illusions that you are not worthy of it, that it is not possible, that it is not available, and to claim it for yourself? This is how you break free from the stories that have been holding you back and from the programming and conditioning that keeps you in a box, that keeps you searching for what you have known was available to you all along.

Your soul would not have the desire if it was not meant for you. Your intuition guides you to highest alignment, to flow, to a life aligned with divine love, but you must listen. It is living your truth that aligns you with love, and it is the frequency of love that shines light on the truth. Illusions and fear cannot hold when divine love is truly present. Are you willing to move past illusions? Are you willing to transmute your fears? This is available to you. Do not forget the power of love—to heal, to transmute, to create. It is an invisible force, a frequency, that moves through all of you—that drives you, motivates you, consumes you. It moves mountains. It sets you free. It makes you question everything you thought you knew. It is an energy that takes many forms—an intangible that is somehow present in all, known by all, and felt by all. You need not see it to know it.

Connection is a key part of your experience, allowing you to know yourself more deeply, and allowing you to connect more deeply with the frequency of divine love. It is time for you to be truly conscious and intentional with the relationships you create. They are central to your life. They are the energetic cords that support you, or do not. When you calibrate your field so all relationships are vibrating at the frequency of divine love, you experience an entire reality of divine love. This is divine! This is ecstasy! This is purpose! This is liberation! This is possibility! This is joy! It is through your relationships that you feel the exchange of love. It is through your relationships that you get to know and experience all of who you are. It is through your relationships that you are shown the places you can continue to expand, grow, and embody more of your authenticity.

You will learn and activate much through connection, but one of the most important lessons you will learn is what you can create when you are anchored into higher frequencies and aligned with your wholeness and authenticity. You will learn the power of divine love. You will see the difference in partnership and connection—you will experience something you didn't know was possible. You will realize that you do not have to have experienced something before in the physical to co-create it in your reality now. You will recognize that loving as your divine self opens up a world of possibilities you never knew when you were trying to "love" from your ego. What a beautiful lesson in shifting your beliefs about what is possible and what is not! If you can think of it, if you can feel it, you can create it. But it all starts with you.

We hope this text has opened your eyes to a new way of relating, of loving, of living, and of recognizing the love within yourself. It is time to redefine relationships for yourself, to break apart the norms, and to set a new standard. You get to be the example of what it looks like to truly lead with love. You get to shift the planet by anchoring in divine love, simply by being your most authentic self. It feels divine to live as love, to choose from love, to act as love, and to commit to divine love in relationships—because it is! Once you taste it, you will feel so good you will never want to go back! And you will realize, it all started with a choice, which then led to a series of choices—to live as the most authentic, highest version of yourself the whole way through. To live as love itself.

Allow love to move through you, and watch as your life expands. Watch as your reality recalibrates. Watch as you bring love and healing to those around you. Watch as you are reconnected to your purpose, passion, and inspiration, simply by being the truest version of yourself. Drop the resistance, and allow your soul to guide you to the flow of miracles. Remember that what you seek is already within. You are divine love.

ABOUT THE
AUTHOR

Christina Rice is an intuitive channel, celebrity energy healer, best-selling author, and founder of Ahai Energy Healing. Her mission is to support freedom-seekers in stepping into their power, creating their dream realities, and living their most authentic, abundant, and aligned lives. Christina works as a bridge between realms, sharing transformational channeled messages from a number of different Ascended Masters and teaching others how to work with energy to create lasting change in their lives.

Christina has helped thousands of people master the energetics of manifestation when it comes to relationships, money, and health through her books, membership, in-person immersions, and powerful online programs. She runs a top-rated spiritual training school, supporting others in developing their own intuitive and energy healing abilities. Christina is also the host of her own podcast, *Multidimensional with Christina the Channel*, and founder of QRTZ, a spiritual lifestyle brand offering high-vibe products for your everyday life. She also supports other leaders in sharing their own paradigm-shifting messages and stories through her publishing house, Golden Hour Publishing. You can find more from Christina at christinathechannel.com.

www.ingramcontent.com/pod-product-compliance
Lightning Source LLC
Chambersburg PA
CBHW061136120626
46546CB00005B/1816